CONTENTS

MOON DUST

by Melanie Berg • yarn The Uncommon Thread: BFL Fingering

The first astronaut footprints are still visible on the moon's surface after nearly 50 years. In the absence of atmosphere and erosion, impressions left on the moon sit undisturbed virtually forever. Melanie's beanie and fingerless mitts set draws on the winding tracks left behind by rickshaws used by astronauts exploring the moon.

Knit in the round with the right side facing inward for painless reverse stocking stitch, Melanie evokes the rocky surface of the illuminated moon in lustrous fingering weight Blue Faced Leicester. Twisted stitches snake across the dunes of your hands and brow to remind us that all great journeys are made up of small steps.

Pattern on page 50.
#moondustbeanie #moondustmitts

LUNA by Anna Strandberg • yarn Dandelion Yarns: Rosy Sport

Luna is the name of both the Roman goddess of the moon and the Space Race Era Soviet moon exploration programme. For Anna's futuristic but feminine pullover, we could conjure no better combination. This is the sweater for sweater-haters and other easily bored knitters. Using brioche in the round and knit from the top down with tailored shoulder detailing, it's mostly knit stitches but with enough fun things going on for a supremely pleasurable knit.

Made with Anna's own hand-dyed organic yarn, it's what Anna says she'd wear if she ever went to the moon. Luna is cheering you on as she charges her silver moon chariot across the night sky!

Pattern on page 55.
#lunapullover

ARTEMIS

Artemis is the ancient huntress, and her Cyclops-forged bow and the waxing crescent moon are her symbols. She helps women through puberty, fertility, childbirth, and motherhood despite remaining a maiden herself. Rather than a nurturer, however, Artemis is a fearsome protector presiding over nature; she famously transfigured a peeping tom into a stag and hunted him down after catching him spying on her bathing in a forest spring.

Designed to be drapey with a scoop back outlined in a glimmering crescent moon, our Artemis is a showstopper. The shoulders are knit separately to shape the neck and back before joining the body in one piece. Sleeves are added top down and golden short rows sculpt the moon detail. Whatever hunting you do in this top, Artemis has your back.

Pattern on page 59.
#artemistop

by Esther Romo • yarn: Shibui Knits: Cima and Silk Cloud | Anchor: Artiste Metallic

HECATE

by **Maddie Harvey** • *yarn* **Woollenflower: Masgot Fine** and **Whorl**

With plant-dyed yarn and a radiant crescent-moon motif, this could be named after no one but Hecate (he-ka-tee), ancient Greek moon goddess of plant magic and sorcery. Altars to Hecate with plant and food offerings were placed at entrances and crossroads under the dark skies of the new moon. Believers hoped she and her ghost hounds would keep watch for restless spirits, as three-bodied Hecate could look in three directions at once, representing the waxing, full, and waning moon.

Maddie's shawl evokes Hecate's crescent peeking through a cloudy night sky. Knit in two parts then finished with contrasting bobbled i-cord edging, the simple slipped-stitch moon motif contrasts in bright mohair lace against an inky stockinette background. This is a shawl for protection, if only from the cold.

Pattern on page 63.
#hecateshawl

CERIDWEN

by Fiona Alice • Yarn Illimani Yarn: Amelie

Moody cables belong to shadowy autumn evenings, whether you spend them trick-or-treating or gathering plants for moon magic. Fiona's relaxed cables hold a hidden message with central honeycomb panels echoing outward from full to crescent moons. The ripple effect reminds us of the keeper of the cauldron of knowledge and inspiration in Welsh folklore. Shapeshifter Ceridwen is mother, enchantress, and crone, personifying wisdom, change, rebirth, and the phases of the moon.

Pom Pom normally champions colour, but the pale mulberry silk core and black baby alpaca halo of Illimani's Amelie has entranced us.

Knit in pieces from the bottom up in an unbelievably lightweight aran, cables and moons flash in luminous highlights with a supernatural combination of softness and stitch definition. Clever Ceridwen must have cooked this one up herself.

Pattern on page 66.
#ceridwenpullover

by Carissa Browning • yarn Madelinetosh: Pashmina

HYPATIA

One of the few moon craters named after a woman sits in the Sea of Tranquility lunar basin, A renowned astronomer, mathematician and philosopher in Byzantine Alexandria, Hypatia ran afoul of religious dogma. She was accused of satanic practices and beguiling politicians through witchcraft, then killed by a mob of Christian monks. It sent shockwaves throughout the Mediterranean, memorialising Hypatia instantly as martyr to knowledge and women's rights.

Carissa's fully reversible cowl is dotted with shadowy craters like Hypatia. Luxurious Pashmina is held double for the background and double knit across the craters, quickly building up the most comforting cowl imaginable. We love this romantically soft tonal contrast, but play around to recreate lunar light effects that speak to you. We think Hypatia would have liked to be remembered by moonlight centuries later.

Pattern on page 71.
#hypatiacowl

SINA

by Amy Philip • *yarn* Triskelion Yarn: Scylfing DK

According to one Polynesian legend, Sina fled an eel god's harassment by exploring the earth in a magical canoe. When she had seen all the earthly shores, she paddled to the moon. It was so tranquil that Sina stayed forever, forming the shadows of the moon and watching over night travellers while weaving bark cloth from her banyan tree.

Worked in the round from the bottom up with a rustic but soft BFL and Gotland blend, the yarn is held double for nippy nights and the second strand is dropped for the half-moon motif on the palm. The shadow half of the moon's face curves around the hand and disappears when you hold your hands together.

Catch moonbeams (or the moon itself!) on your travels and find yourself at home in the unexpected.

Pattern on page 74.
#sinamittens

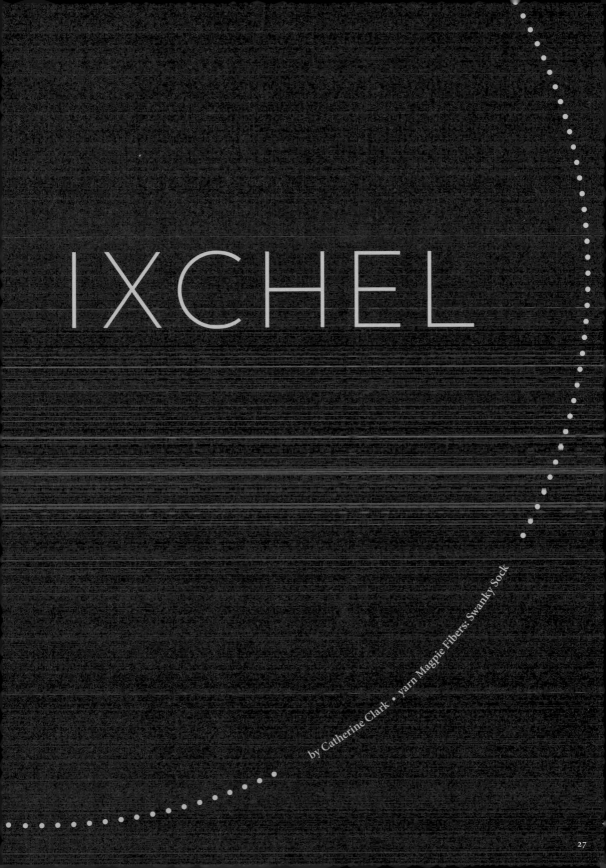

IXCHEL

by Catherine Clark • yarn Magpie Fibers: Swanky Sock

Ixchel (ee-SHELL) is the ancient Mayan jaguar
goddess of rainbows and childbirth, a medicine
woman, and midwife who protects against disease and
grants fertility. Few details survived the conquistadors,
but her temple at Cozumel was a pilgrimage site
for Mayan women. Some say Ixchel changes from
maiden to crone with the phases of the moon and
others say she lives in its shadows.

More than a sweater, Catherine has designed a knitted
ode to the transformational powers shared between
women and the moon. The shape follows the body
like a favourite t-shirt, knit from the top down with
colourwork yoke. Stars and lunar charts adorn every
surface, with stars fading down the body. The full
moon is centred over the solar plexus for healing
energy whenever you need it, whatever phase of life
you are in.

Pattern on page 78.
#ixchelpullover

SKY MAP

Sky Map began as a story on Canadian radio, where astronaut Nicole Stott described her first experience of being surrounded by space after a lifetime of seeing the sky as though flat from Earth. The astronaut's description of the vast expanses viewed against the smallness of our earth and moon encouraged Emily to explore the idea of being wrapped up in space.

Knit as a long stockinette tube in Emily's own heavenly Viola Mohair Lace, the stole is anchored into a rectangle by embroidering a scattering of stars, constellations, planets and moons in high-contrast yarn across it. Experienced embroiderers can get as fancy as they like but, with no rigid layout, fuzzy imperfections give this sky its otherworldly charm. Even the least experienced embroiderer can feel brave enough to launch themselves into this night sky.

Pattern on page 84.
#skymapwrap

MOONBOW

Jule made friends with the moon when she moved to the north German countryside. Away from Berlin's lights, she discovered moonbeams bright enough to guide her evening walks, illuminating an enigmatic palette of nighttime colours that she poured into Hey Mama Wolf yarns. The rustling moonlit branches and grasses of Jule's nocturnal garden inspired the fringe detailing of this bold but totally wearable design.

Constructed in pieces with a combination of raglans and saddle shoulders for a structured but modern fit, the arched fringe and restrained ombre reminded us of moonbows. This rare nocturnal phenomenon of silvery white or lilac rainbows can only be seen under a full moon, if you are lucky enough to find the perfect combination of fog, mist, seaspray, and physics.

Pattern on page 88.
#moonbowpullover

by Jule Kebelmann • yarn Hey Mama Wolf: Schafwolle No.03 and Sockyarn No.04

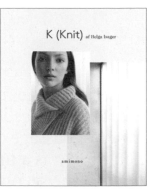

PICTURING MANY MOONS

Like the cycles of the moon, stitches make an excellent marker of the passage of time. Each stitch is a unit, equivalent to the seconds it took to shape. When knitting in the round, we even make ourselves an alternative clock face that our hands travel round, leaving behind them indelible marks of minutes, and then hours, passed in stitches. The stitches we form are a beautiful manifestation of time, the benefits of age, and the acquired knowledge for shaping them. So why is it that these accumulated years are not celebrated, but derided in jokes about older women and caricatures of grandmothers? And why is ageing absent from the majority of images presented to us?

words by **Anna Maltz**
illustration by **Sandra Eterovic**

'Knitting isn't just for grandmothers' is a very true statement in one sense, yet it often carries the implication that an activity associated with older women needs reclaiming or reinventing to make it relevant to others. Who decides what constitutes 'old' anyway? It is an elastic term. On a personal level, it shifts constantly in relation to our own age and those in our orbit. When you're five, eight is old. When you are 58, 85 is old. When I was 5, my grandmother seemed old at 70; I'm now aged 39, and my 70-year-old mother still seems young. All my grandparents died at around 84, so while I am not old old, I am now halfway there by my family's standards. My current circumstances dictate that I will never be a grandmother, so I will not be able to use that title as a marker of true oldness. On a cultural level, old age is also flexible, expanding or contracting in relation to what and whom it is describing, as well as fluctuating with historical and geographical variations in life expectancy.

If 'grandmother' is being used as a stand-in term for 'old woman', perhaps it is useful to look at when a woman can become a grandmother as a marker of what that term can mean – bearing in mind that becoming a grandmother is an involuntary act. Let's observe the UK age of consent, which dictates that sexual intercourse of the sort that can produce a baby is legal from the age of 16. Then, taking human gestation periods into account, this means that you could be a grandmother at 33. This probably isn't the age most of us imagine when we think about grandmothers knitting. It is likely that we are picturing someone at least double that age, and a caricature at that.

Older women who knit, whether or not they are caricatured as 'grandmothers', are without doubt many moons older than the women that typically appear on knitting social media, or the models, professional or otherwise, we see pictured in knitting patterns. Knitting unites ages, and allows many occasions for intergenerational friendship, support and the exchange of knowledge through a levelling shared interest. However, there is a bias towards youth in the images produced by the knitting world as a whole, whether by knitters or businesses. The pictures that we see, and post ourselves on social media, are important, because as the the old adage says, seeing is believing.

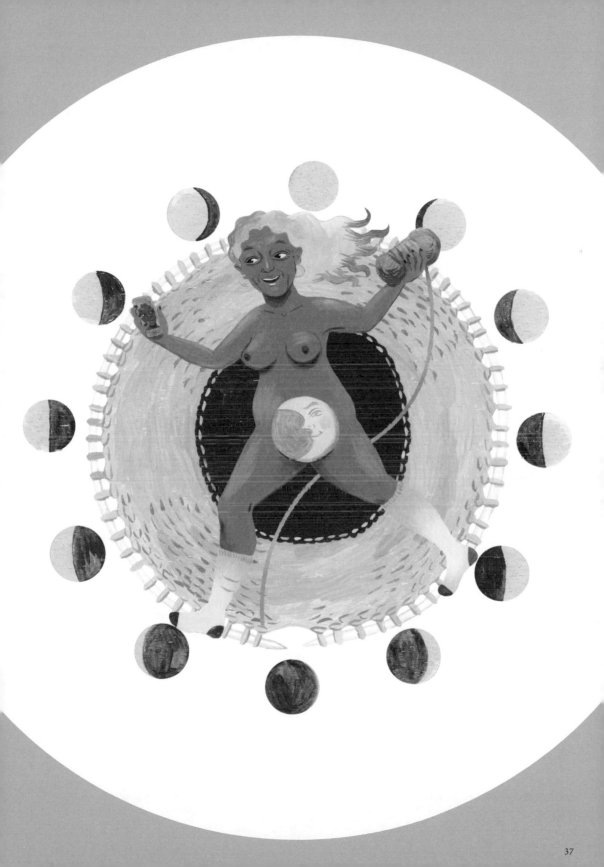

Businesses certainly still rely heavily on the standard dogma of youth-worship in advertising. A change is overdue, and likely to happen slowly, but we can hurry it along by actively supporting more age-diverse imagery with equal likes, shares and purchases. The number of knitting designers who model for their own patterns dwindles dramatically among the over 40s crowd and falls off even more dramatically among the over 50s. I think this will change as the designers who found their stride during the Ravelry-led transformation of the knitting world continue to self-publish and model their own designs. They already seem at ease with being inextricably bound with their own branding, so one can only hope that we will have the joy of ageing along with them.

Knitters are a smart bunch but that doesn't mean we currently have the capacity to instantly shed years of being influenced by the advertising industry insidiously telling us what type of pictures sell products. While we may want to see our own diverse selves reflected, we may not yet be in a position to actually perceive such images as anything more than a novelty, open to judgement in a way that images of 'standard' models are not. But we can work on this by supporting those who are already making the change and joining in ourselves. There might be an element of being sacrificial mutton, but social change relies on brave souls to push for it by being the change they want to see.

Away from the narrow frame of companies' images, swathes of society have been turning the camera on themselves. While selfies are easily associated with the presumptive vapidity of youth, they are building up an entire catalogue of diversity. As the selfie generation ages, I hope they will continue to photograph themselves and thereby help remove some of the stigmas of age, making it visible where others have made it invisible – partly because the technology did not exist, and partly because of the flawed idea that old age is at odds with beauty.

This burden cannot be shrugged off without a formal and informal stock of images containing older people. Unfortunately, older women tend to edit themselves out. This may be down to shyness, or to satisfy personal needs for privacy, but it will not help to chivvy things along. The tools we need to share and praise images are already in our hands.

When I was a child, the superhero power I was most curious about was invisibility. I spent a lot of time considering it and the associated pros and cons. Would I be able to switch my invisibility on and off, or would it be a permanent condition? At what point would the things I came in contact with (such as food and clothing) become invisible too? And, being practical, I wondered whether my poo would be invisible or visible, once it left my body. When I felt awkward as a teen, the ability to disappear would often have been desirable. It was at this age that I was regularly told by older people that one day I would look back on pictures of myself, recognise my own beauty and aspire to such youth. In my mid-20s, I did a lot of work around making knitting invisible without erasing it (no frogging or burning). This resulted in a series of chromakey blue knits that could become invisible in a blue-screen studio. I did a lot of accompanying research into how invisibility is represented in film and television. I found that it is usually something that men acquire in order to do unpleasant things such as breaking and entering, murder, theft, or just plain creeping around. Now I find myself at an age when I am regularly told that, as a woman, I will become invisible when I turn 50. To my teenage self, this sounds not entirely unappealing, but it is rarely presented as such.

AGEING HAPPENS TO US ALL, WITH EVERY PASSING STITCH, MINUTE, AND MOONRISE

If we want to counteract this invisibility, and see more older women in pictures and advertising, we will have to start taking pictures of ourselves more, because then the market can follow trodden paths, as it prefers to do. It is not fair to take ourselves out of the picture and expect others to put us back in. There are shining exceptions, but so much more can be done. Older women – please share images of yourselves! If duck lips, peace fingers and belfies don't appeal, then find something that does. Advanced Style has achieved a lot by celebrating the beauty and joy of dressing up in older age, but it is still largely based on novelty and flamboyance. What we need is for it to become normal. Normal can still be a celebration and contain as much diversity for older people as it does for younger people's fashion. Yes, yarn companies, designers and magazines do have a responsibility to show diversity in their models in order for things to progress, but that responsibility also lies in the less-youthful among us sharing pictures of ourselves, and in all of our reactions to images of diversity.

Ageing happens to us all, with every passing stitch, minute, and moonrise, regardless of race, gender identity, body size and physical ability. As inevitably as our projects grow and our knitting knowledge develops, so too does our age. Ageing is glorious; it is progress. It is something we should and can celebrate by taking, embracing and promoting images of those who would otherwise be invisible.

SHOOT
FOR THE
MOON

Behind the scenes in Mooresburg

words by **Lydia Gluck, Meghan Fernandes + Sophie Scott**
images by **Meghan Fernandes**

When musing on the theme, colours, and textures of a new Pom Pom publication, the location of a photoshoot is one of the fundamental elements in capturing the character of the knits. So, in February 2018 the team travelled to the tiny town of Mooresburg, Canada to visit a very special dye studio: the 100-year-old general store where Emily Foden, the alchemist behind Viola Yarns, lives and works. Already full of rich history, this beautiful space is now also the inspiration and location for her forthcoming pattern book *Knits About Winter*, published by Pom Pom Press.

Editors Meghan Fernandes and Lydia Gluck interview each other and reflect on the snow, sunsets, and skeins that made this memorable shoot.

Meghan: How did you feel about travelling so far for the first time for a shoot (to a place other than where we each live)?

Lydia: It felt like an exciting step to take, but one that made a lot of sense. We felt it was so important to get a sense of the landscape that inspired so much of Emily's work since she moved to Mooresburg that it would have felt wrong to shoot anywhere else. Also we were all very keen that snow should feature in the photography, and of course neither Austin nor London are really known for their abundance of snow, especially not of the sort we got to experience in Mooresburg. I also felt privileged to be able to spend that time in Mooresburg and get to know the area a little; it helped us to better understand the book and where it was going. So I felt overall that it was a series of sensible decisions that led us there, but also that I was incredibly lucky to be in that place and time, with such wonderful people, and among such inspiring things.

M: Everything at Emily's home and studio seems to have an air of magic about it - what were your favourite things about the place?

L: It's true that it is a magical place. One of my favourite things was the light in the living room where the shop would have been when it was still a general store. The fact that there were huge windows meant that the natural light was a real presence throughout the day. It's a lovely feeling to be able to see the sky constantly, while still being cosy.

M: We often end up swooning over a new colour or a particular dye lot of Emily's yarn - what do you think makes her dyeing so special?

L: Having seen Emily dye, it's no surprise to me that her colourways are so unique. Emily sees colour in a way that is hard to describe, and she works carefully on recreating the colourscapes that inspire her. It seems that she is never quite finished, she's constantly tweaking and changing her colours, and that feeling of possibility really comes through.

It's fair to say that Emily is often inspired by nature, and that the colours she creates come from her perception of the landscape around her. I think what Emily captures is the real diversity and depth of colour that we see around us. For Emily brown is never just brown. On top of her lovely semi-solid dyeing she adds layers of colour, and then her trademark sparse speckles – often in unlikely contrasts. Sometimes her combinations can at first look unusual, but now that I'm more familiar with the way she works I can see how she has drawn together the colours you might see for example in a tree, and knowing Emily, it's probably a very specific tree that she has watched over time. I don't want to speak for her because I haven't actually asked her about this, but when I look at her colours I can see little worlds and landscapes, and I am drawn to them because they are at once of the natural world – more so than a lot of dyeing because of the range and subtlety of the colours – and otherworldly, like a glimpse of something that you have never seen before.

M: What is one of your loveliest memories of the week in Mooresburg?

L: It's so hard to choose… what a nice problem to have! I think I am torn between the lovely snowy bonfire we had on our last night there, and seeing the sunrise on the last morning. The bonfire felt like a culmination of our week in Mooresburg. We had all got to know each other better by then, and it did feel like a celebratory moment. We had finished shooting and we were all happy with the images, so that was a weight off our minds, and we could concentrate more fully on just enjoying the surroundings. It was also a real novelty to have a bonfire in the snow! All wrapped up in our coats, making s'mores and hearing all sorts of tales (bears and camping and sledding – oh my!). It really was a once-in-a-lifetime experience. But the sunrise on our last morning stands out for me too. During our stay I became a little obsessed with seeing the sunrise – which the jet-lag definitely helped! On the last morning there was

still lots of snow on the ground, and I ran outside to try and take a picture of the colours of the sky as the sun came up. My hair was still wet but I didn't want to wait. When I got out there I realised that any pictures I took could never do it justice so I just stood and watched the colours for as long as I could before I got too cold. When I got back inside my hair was frozen, which was a first for me, and it felt so nice to be warm inside again, but still with the glow of the sunrise filling my mind.

L: There was a lot of snow around while we were in Mooresburg (which was perfect for the shoot) - what was your favourite snowy moment?

M: Oh there was so much snow! I am like a little kid when it snows, still. And we were not disappointed. Up there in the top moments has to be our sleigh ride. Emily arranged for us to be taken on a horse-drawn sleigh by her neighbour, Maria. Seeing the vast snowy landscape like this was exhilarating and breathtaking, not to mention straight out of a fairy tale. Our walk up to Emily's neighbours' property, Skyhill, on our last night was also so, so beautiful. We could see the sun setting between the trees from atop the hill and I couldn't stop taking photos. Every few steps presented another stunning peachy, coral, golden perspective.

L: The food we ate during our stay was pretty amazing! Did you have a favourite meal and why?

M: Food is so important, isn't it? And Emily and her family had prepared for our visit so well, making soups and stews and granola and all manner of wonderful, hearty things. I don't know if just one meal stands out for me, but I know I will never forget how we prepared for every lunch and dinner all together, clearing and setting the table, pouring wine, and sitting together by candlelight, or beside the huge windows with the snow falling outside. We could have sat there forever if there hadn't been a book to shoot. I will also never forget the maple sausage rolls I bought in town - in my opinion one of Canada's greatest ever contributions to the world, second only to Emily's yarn.

L: What inspiration did you take from the trip to Mooresburg that you have been able to use in your making since then?

M: The trip certainly made me long for colder weather in Austin! Emily's colours and designs can't help but make you welcome and embrace winter. I am astounded by how her colours can lean towards pastel but at the same time have the warmth you might long for in the colder months. And of course her use of different fibres and colours held together has opened up a whole new dimension for me. What would a golden mohair look like paired with a rustic purple wool? Magic, that's what.

L: When you think of the week we spent in Mooresburg, what is the moment or image that stands out most in your mind?

M: Every day was beautiful, alternating between soft, fluttering snow and brilliant sunshine, and bookended by a slow and glorious sunrise and a stunning photo-worthy sunset. I think overall I will remember the hospitality of Emily and her family and friends in the beautiful surroundings, both natural and of their making: Emily's mum's calligraphic handwriting on the spice jars; little star garlands in the bathroom; perfectly imperfect shelves full of packaging materials; cream decanted into a ceramic jug to have with coffee. I think that all these special little touches, and the magic of the surrounding landscape, have somehow made it into the pages of the book we went there to work on. At least I hope we have done it all justice!

Knits About Winter is due for release October 2018.

PATTERNS

Abbreviations & Techniques

beg	Beginning
cast off	Bind off
dec	Decrease
DPN(s)	Double-pointed needle(s)
foll	Follow(s)/Following
G st	Garter stitch
inc	Increase
k	Knit
kfb	Knit into the front and back of a stitch
kbf	Knit into the back then into the front of a stitch
k2tog	Knit 2 stitches together
k3tog	Knit 3 stitches together
LH	Left hand
M1	Work as M1L
M1L	Make 1 Left; pick up strand between the two needles from the front to back with the tip of left needle, knit into the back of this stitch
M1R	Make 1 Right; pick up strand between the two needles from back to front with the tip of left needle, knit into the front of this stitch
M1P	Work as M1LP
M1LP	Make 1 Left Purlwise; pick up strand between the two needles from front to back with the tip of left needle, purl into the back of this stitch
M1RP	Make 1 Right Purlwise; pick up strand between the two needles from back to front with the tip of left needle, purl into the front of this stitch
patt	Pattern
PM	Place marker
p	Purl
pfb	Purl into the front and back of a stitch
p2tog	Purl 2 stitches together
rem	Remain(s)/Remaining
rep	Repeat
rev St st	Reverse Stocking stitch (stockinette): purl on RS rows, knit on WS rows
RH	Right hand
RS	Right side of fabric
sl	Slip
s2kpo	Slip 2 stitches together knitwise, knit next stitch, pass slipped stitches over

sk2po	Slip 1 stitch knitwise, knit next 2 stitches together, pass slipped stitch over
ssk	Slip 2 stitches knitwise one at a time, knit together through the back loops
sssk	Slip 3 stitches knitwise one at a time, knit together through the back loops
ssp	Slip 2 stitches knitwise one at a time, purl together through the back loops
SM	Slip marker
st(s)	Stitch(es)
St st	Stocking stitch (stockinette): knit on RS rows, purl on WS rows
tbl	Through the back loop
tog	Together
wyib	With yarn held in back of work
wyif	With yarn held in front of work
w&t	Wrap and turn: On RS rows, move yarn to front, sl st from left needle to right needle, turn. On WS rows, move yarn to back, sl st from left needle to right needle, move yarn to front, sl st back to left needle, turn.
WS	Wrong side of fabric
yo	Yarn over needle and into working position

The following Pom Pom tutorials are available for techniques used in this issue:

3-needle cast off and video at http://bit.ly/2cqw9yT	Issue 5
Backwards loop cast on	Issue 13
Cabling without a cable needle	Issue 6
I-cord	Issue 13
Long-tail cast on	Issue 11
Wrap and turn	Issue 10

INTRODUCING

ECO-CASHMERE

50% RECYCLED CASHMERE/50% VIRGIN CASHMERE

MADE IN ITALY

Moondust Beanie
by Melanie Berg

Sizes: 1 (2, 3)
Finished circumference: 43 (47, 51) cm / 17 (18½, 20)"
Model wears size 2.
Yarn: The Uncommon Thread BFL Fingering (4ply/
Fingering; 100% wool, 402 m / 440 yds per 100 g skein)
Shade: Lark; 1 skein
Gauge: 27 sts & 40 rows = 10 cm / 4" in reverse stocking
stitch on 3.5 mm needles after blocking.
Needles: 3.5 mm / US 4 knitting needles suitable for
working small circumferences in the round
Always use a needle size that will result in the correct
gauge after blocking.
Notions: 1 cable needle, 5 stitch markers
Notes: The Moondust hat is worked in the round with
the WS facing you for ease of knitting. Please read
through the entire pattern to familiarise yourself with
its construction before starting to knit.

Stitch Glossary

Note: As the hat is worked with the WS facing
throughout, all cables are worked using purl stitches.
1/1 LC: Sl 1 st to cable needle and hold in front, p1, p1
from cable needle
1/1 RC: Sl 1 st to cable needle and hold in back, p1, p1
from cable needle
1/2 LC: Sl 2 sts to cable needle and hold in front, p1, p2
from cable needle
1/2 RC: Sl 1 st to cable needle and hold in back, p2, p1
from cable needle

PATTERN BEGINS

Using the long-tail method, cast on 116 (126, 136) sts.
Join for knitting in the round, being careful not to twist.
PM to indicate beg of round. **Note:** the **WS** of hat will
be facing throughout.
Round 1: [K1, p1tbl] to end.
Rep round 1 a further 18 (20, 22) times.
Next round: [K1, p1tbl] to last 2 sts, k2tog. *115 (125, 135) sts*

Begin Textured Pattern

Rounds 1-2: K2, [k3, p3] twice, k to end.
Round 3: K2, [k3, 1/2 LC] twice, k to end.
Round 4: K2, [k2, 1/1 LC, k2] twice, k to end.
Round 5: K2, [1/2 LC, k3] twice, k to end.
Rounds 6-8: K2, [p3, k3] twice, k to end.
Round 9: K2, [1/2 RC, k3] twice, k to end.
Round 10: K2, [k2, 1/1 RC, k2] twice, k to end.
Round 11: K2, [k3, 1/2 RC] twice, k to end.
Round 12: Rep round 1.
Rep rounds 1-12 a further 3 times then rounds 1-11
once more.
Next round: Rep round 12 and **AT THE SAME TIME**
place markers for shaping as foll: *patt across 23 (25, 27)
sts, PM; rep from * three times, patt to end.
Note: 5 markers are placed in total, including beg of
round marker.

Shape crown

Round 1: K2, [k3, p3] twice, [k to 2 sts before marker,
k2tog] 5 times. *110 (120, 130) sts*
Round 2: K2, [k3, p3] twice, k to end.
Round 3: K2, [k3, 1/2 LC] twice, [k to 2 sts before marker,
k2tog] 5 times. *105 (115, 125) sts*
Round 4: K2, [k2, 1/1 LC, k2] twice, k to end.
Round 5: K2, [1/2 LC, k3] twice, [k to 2 sts before marker,
k2tog] 5 times. *100 (110, 120) sts*
Round 6: K2, [p3, k3] twice, k to end.
Round 7: K2, [p3, k3] twice, [k to 2 sts before marker,
k2tog] 5 times. *95 (105, 115) sts*
Round 8: K2, [p3, k3] twice, k to end.
Round 9: K2, [1/2 RC, k3] twice, [k to 2 sts before
marker, k2tog] 5 times. *90 (100, 110) sts*
Round 10: K2, [k2, 1/1 RC, k2] twice, k to end.
Round 11: K2, [k3, 1/2 RC] twice, [k to 2 sts before
marker, k2tog] 5 times. *85 (95, 105) sts*
Round 12: K2, [k3, p3] twice, k to end.
Round 13: K2, [k3, p3] twice, [k to 2 sts before marker,
k2tog] 5 times. *80 (90, 100) sts*
Round 14: K2, [k3, p3] twice, [k to 2 sts before marker,
k2tog] 5 times. *75 (85, 95) sts*

Moondust Beanie
by Melanie Berg

Size 1 ONLY

Round 15: K5, p3, k3, p2, k2tog, SM, [k to 2 sts before marker, k2tog] 4 times. *70 sts*

Round 16: K5, p3, k3, p1, k2tog, SM, [k to 2 sts before marker, k2tog] 4 times. *65 sts*

Round 17: K5, p3, k3, k2tog, SM, [k to 2 sts before marker, k2tog] 4 times. *60 sts*

Round 18: K5, p3, k2, k2tog, SM, [k to 2 sts before marker, k2tog] 4 times. *55 sts*

Round 19: K5, p3, k1, k2tog, SM, [k to 2 sts before marker, k2tog] 4 times. *50 sts*

Round 20: K5, p3, k2tog, SM, [k to 2 sts before marker, k2tog] 4 times. *45 sts*

Round 21: K5, p2, k2tog, SM, [k to 2 sts before marker, k2tog] 4 times. *40 sts*

Round 22: K5, p1, k2tog, SM, [k to 2 sts before marker, k2tog] 4 times. *35 sts*

Round 23: [K to 2 sts before marker, k2tog] 5 times. *30 sts*

Round 24: [K to 2 sts before marker, k2tog] 5 times. *25 sts*

Round 25: Removing markers, k2tog eleven times, k3tog. *12 sts*

Round 26: K2tog six times. *6 sts*

Size 2 ONLY

Round 15: K2, [k3, 1/2 LC] twice, [k to 2 sts before marker, k2tog] 5 times. *80 sts*

Round 16: K2, [k2, 1/1 LC, k2] twice, [k to 2 sts before marker, k2tog] 5 times. *75 sts*

Round 17: K2, 1/2 LC, k3, 1/2 LC, k2, k2tog, SM, [k to 2 sts before marker, k2tog] 4 times. *70 sts*

Round 18: K2, p3, k3, p3, k1, k2tog, SM, [k to 2 sts before marker, k2tog] 4 times. *65 sts*

Round 19: K2, p3, k3, p3, k2tog, SM, [k to 2 sts before marker, k2tog] 4 times. *60 sts*

Round 20: K2, p3, k3, p2, k2tog, SM, [k to 2 sts before marker, k2tog] 4 times. *55 sts*

Round 21: K2, p3, k3, p1, k2tog, SM, [k to 2 sts before marker, k2tog] 4 times. *50 sts*

Round 22: K2, p3, k3, k2tog, SM, [k to 2 sts before marker, k2tog] 4 times. *45 sts*

Round 23: K2, p3, k2, k2tog, SM, [k to 2 sts before marker, k2tog] 4 times. *40 sts*

Round 24: K2, p3, k1, k2tog, SM, [k to 2 sts before marker, k2tog] 4 times. *35 sts*

Inspirational artisan yarns from the USA
figtreeyarns.co.uk

Moondust Beanie
by Melanie Berg

Round 25: K2, p3, k2tog, SM, [k to 2 sts before marker, k2tog] 4 times. *30 sts*
Round 26: K2, p2, k2tog, SM, [k to 2 sts before marker, k2tog] 4 times. *25 sts*
Round 27: Removing markers, k2tog eleven times, k3tog. *12 sts*
Round 28: K2tog six times. *6 sts*

Size 3 ONLY
Round 15: K2, [k3, 1/2 LC] twice, [k to 2 sts before marker, k2tog] 5 times. *90 sts*
Round 16: K2, [k2, 1/1 LC, k2] twice, [k to 2 sts before marker, k2tog] 5 times. *85 sts*
Round 17: K2, [1/2 LC, k3] twice, [k to 2 sts before marker, k2tog] 5 times. *80 sts*
Round 18: K2, [p3, k3] twice, [k to 2 sts before marker, k2tog] 5 times. *75 sts*
Round 19: K2, p3, k3, p3, k2, k2tog, SM, [k to 2 sts before marker, k2tog] 4 times. *70 sts*
Round 20: K2, p3, k3, p3, k1, k2tog, SM, [k to 2 sts before marker, k2tog] 4 times. *65 sts*
Round 21: K2, 1/2 RC, k3, p3, k2tog, SM, [k to 2 sts before marker, k2tog] 4 times. *60 sts*

Round 22: K4, 1/1 RC, k4, k2tog, SM, [k to 2 sts before marker, k2tog] 4 times. *55 sts*
Round 23: K5, 1/2 RC, k1, k2tog, SM, [k to 2 sts before marker, k2tog] 4 times. *50 sts*
Round 24: K5, p3, k2tog, SM, [k to 2 sts before marker, k2tog] 4 times. *45 sts*
Round 25: K5, p2, k2tog, SM, [k to 2 sts before marker, k2tog] 4 times. *40 sts*
Round 26: K5, p1, k2tog, SM, [k to 2 sts before marker, k2tog] 4 times. *35 sts*
Round 27: [K to 2 sts before marker, k2tog] 5 times. *30 sts*
Round 28: [K to 2 sts before marker, k2tog] 5 times. *25 sts*
Round 29: K2tog eleven times, k3tog. *12 sts*
Round 30: K2tog six times. *6 sts*

ALL sizes again
Cut yarn and pull through last 6 sts.

FINISHING
Weave in ends. Wash and block gently.

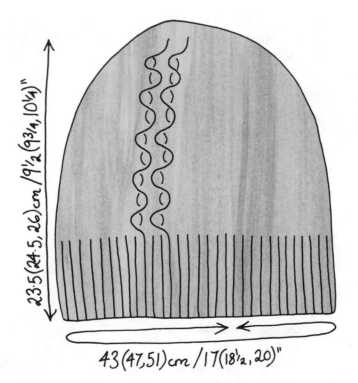

23.5(24.5, 26)cm /9½ (9¾, 10¼)"

43(47,51)cm / 17(18½, 20)"

Moondust Mitts
by Melanie Berg

Sizes: 1 (2, 3)
Finished circumference: 16 (17.5, 18.5) cm / 6¼ (7, 7¼)"
Model wears size 2.
Yarn: The Uncommon Thread BFL Fingering (4ply/
Fingering weight; 100% wool, 402 m / 440 yds per 100 g skein)
Shade: Lark; 1 skein
Gauge: 30 sts & 40 rows = 10 cm / 4" over reverse stocking
stitch on 3.5 mm needles after blocking.
Needles: 3.5 mm / US 4 knitting needles suitable for
working small circumferences in the round
Always use a needle size that will result in the correct
gauge after blocking.
Notions: 1 stitch marker, cable needle, stitch holder or
scrap yarn
Notes: The Moondust mitts are worked in the round
with the WS facing you for ease of knitting. Please read
through the entire pattern to familiarise yourself with its
construction before starting to knit.

Stitch Glossary
Note: As the mitts are worked with the WS facing
throughout, all cables are worked using purl stitches.
1/1 LC: Sl 1 st to cable needle and hold in front, p1, p1
from cable needle
1/1 RC: Sl 1 st to cable needle and hold in back, p1, p1
from cable needle

1/2 LC: Sl 2 sts to cable needle and hold in front, p1, p2
from cable needle
1/2 RC: Sl 1 st to cable needle and hold in back, p2, p1
from cable needle

Textured Pattern - Left Mitt ONLY
Rounds 1-2: K4, [k3, p3] twice, k to end.
Round 3: K4, [k3, 1/2 LC] twice, k to end.
Round 4: K4, [k2, 1/1 LC, k2] twice, k to end.
Round 5: K4, [1/2 LC, k3] twice, k to end.
Rounds 6-8: K4, [p3, k3] twice, k to end.
Round 9: K4, [1/2 RC, k3] twice, k to end.
Round 10: K4, [k2, 1/1 RC, k2] twice, k to end.
Round 11: K4, [k3, 1/2 RC] twice, k to end.
Round 12: Same as round 1.

Textured Pattern - Right Mitt ONLY
Rounds 1-2: K32 (36, 40), [k3, p3] twice, k to end.
Round 3: K32 (36, 40), [k3, 1/2 LC] twice, k to end.
Round 4: K32 (36, 40), [k2, 1/1 LC, k2] twice, k to end.
Round 5: K32 (36, 40), [1/2 LC, k3] twice, k to end.
Rounds 6-8: K32 (36, 40), [p3, k3] twice, k to end.
Round 9: K32 (36, 40), [1/2 RC, k3] twice, k to end.
Round 10: K32 (36, 40), [k2, 1/1 RC, k2] twice, k to end.
Round 11: K32 (36, 40), [k3, 1/2 RC] twice, k to end.
Round 12: Same as round 1.

Moondust Mitts
by **Melanie Berg**

PATTERN BEGINS
RIGHT MITT
Using the long-tail method, cast on 48 (52, 56) sts. Join for knitting in the round, being careful not to twist. PM to indicate beg of round. **Note:** the WS of the mitts will be facing throughout.

Lower hem
Round 1: [K1, p1tbl] to end.
Rep round 1 a further 14 (14, 17) times.

Textured Pattern
Work rounds 1-12 of Textured Pattern 3 times, following correct instructions for Right Mitt.

Thumb gusset
Round 1: M1L, PM, work round 1 of Textured Pattern.
1 thumb st inc; 49 (53, 57) sts
Rounds 2-3: K to marker, SM, work next round of Textured Pattern as set.
Round 4: M1R, k to marker, M1L, SM, work next round of Textured Pattern as set. *2 thumb sts inc*
Rep last 3 rounds a further 5 times, working next round of Textured Pattern each time as set. *61 (65, 69) sts; 13 thumb sts*

Next round: Place 13 sts on stitch holder or scrap yarn for thumb, removing marker, work next round of Textured Pattern as set. *48 (52, 56) sts*

Work straight in Textured Pattern as set for 18 rounds, ending with round 1 of pattern.

Upper hem
Next round: [K1, p1tbl] to end.
Rep last round a further 7 (7, 9) times.
Cast off.

Thumb
Return 13 held thumb sts to working needles, without knitting pick up 5 sts in the gap. *18 sts*
Rejoin yarn to beg of held sts. PM to indicate beg of round.

Size 1 and 2 ONLY
Round 1: K across 13 held sts, k2tog, k1, k2tog. *16 sts*

ALL sizes again
Knit 7 rounds.
Next round: [K1, p1tbl] to end.
Rep last round a further 4 (4, 6) times.
Cast off.

LEFT MITT
Work as for Right Mitt, following Left Mitt Textured Pattern.

FINISHING
Weave in all ends. Wash and block gently.

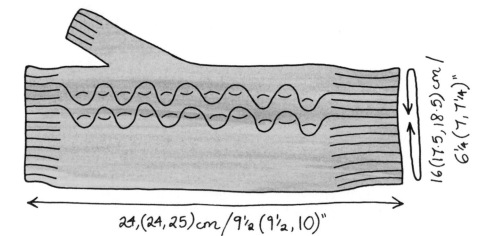

16 (17.5, 18.5) cm / 6¼ (7, 7¼)"

24 (24, 25) cm / 9½ (9½, 10)"

Luna
by Anna Strandberg

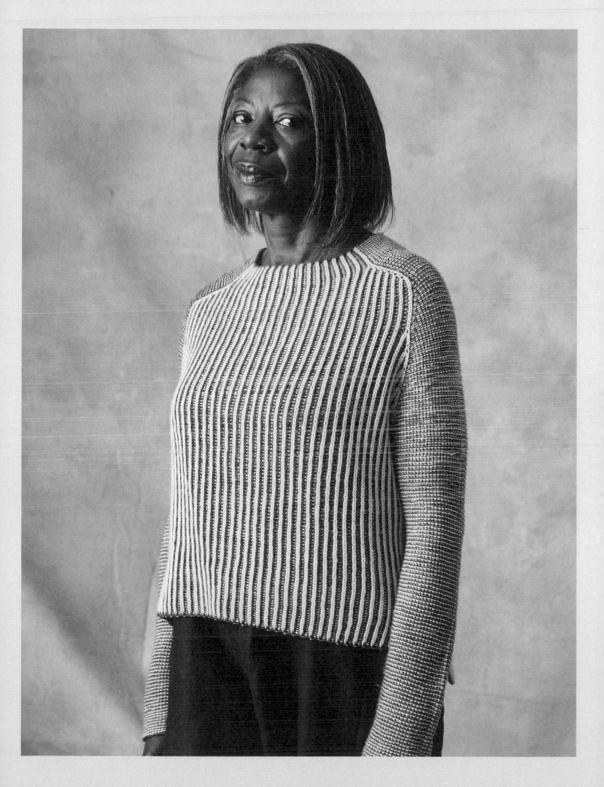

Luna
by Anna Strandberg

Sizes: 1 (2, 3, 4, 5)

Finished bust circumference: 92 (103.5, 113, 124.5, 136.5) cm / 36¼ (40¾, 44½, 49, 53¾)" – to be worn with 15-20 cm / 6-8" positive ease

Model has 94 cm / 37" bust, stands 170 cm / 5'7" tall, and is wearing a size 3.

Yarn: Dandelion Yarns Rosy Sport (sport weight; 100% organic Merino wool; 320 m / 350 yds per 100 g skein)

Shades:

Yarn A: Delicate Feather; 2 (2, 3, 3, 3) skeins

Yarn B: Infinite Universe; 2 (2, 3, 3, 3) skeins

Gauge: 22 sts & 50 rows = 10 cm / 4" over garter stitch on 3.5 mm needles after blocking.

17 sts & 58 rows = 10 cm / 4" over brioche stitch on 3.5 mm needles after blocking.

Needles: 3.5 mm / US 4 circular needle, 80-100 cm / 32-40" length

3 mm / US 2.5 circular needle, 80-100 cm / 32-40" length

Always use a needle size that will result in the correct gauge after blocking.

Notions: 4 stitch markers (1 unique for beg of round), stitch holders or scrap yarn

Note: Use as fine markers as possible.

Notes: Luna is worked from the top down, in the round. Rounds are worked once with yarn A and once with yarn B – the yarn to use for each round is indicated in brackets. Do not twist the yarns together at the beginning of each round. On the last stitch on yarn B rounds, ensure the yarn A yo of the final sl1yo of the previous round remains in place as you work the stitch.

Stitch Glossary

Brk: Knit the sl st and its yo together.

Brp: Purl the sl st and its yo together.

Brkyobrk: Brk into st but leave st on needle, yo, brk into same st, remove st from needle. *2 sts inc*

Inv-R: Pick up the yarn B bump immediately under st just worked on RH needle and knit it. *1 st inc*

Inv-L: Pick up the yarn B bump immediately below next st on LH needle and knit it. *1 st inc*

sl1yo: With yarn in front, sl 1 st pwise, yo. The sl1yo is treated as one stitch.

Elastic Cast Off: K1tbl, p1, sl 2 sts just worked back to LH needle and p2tog, *k1tbl, sl 2 sts from RH needle to LH needle and k2tog tbl, p1, sl 2 sts from RH needle to LH needle and p2tog; rep from * until 1 st rem on RH needle. Break yarn and draw tail through final st to fasten off.

PATTERN BEGINS
YOKE

Using larger needles, yarn B and the German twisted cast on method, cast on 17 (14, 16, 16, 18) sts, PM, cast on 33 (35, 37, 39, 39) sts, PM, cast on 17 (14, 16, 16, 18) sts, PM, cast on 33 (35, 37, 39, 39) sts. *100 (98, 106, 110, 114) sts cast on in total*

Do not turn, change to smaller needles.

Slide all sts to other end of needle, and join yarn A:

Round 1 (A): K to marker, SM, [k1, sl1yo] to last st before marker, k1, SM, k to marker, SM, [k1, sl1yo] to last st, k1. Join to work in the round, being careful not to twist. PM to indicate beg of round.

Round 1 (B): *P to marker, SM, [sl1yo, brp1] to last st before marker, sl1yo, SM; rep from * once more.

Round 2 (A): *K to marker, SM, [brk1, sl1yo] to last st before marker, brk1, SM; rep from * once more.

Round 2 (B): *P to marker, SM, [sl1yo, brp1] to last st before marker, sl1yo, SM; rep from * once more.

Rep round 2 (A and B) a further 13 times. *30 rounds worked in total.*

Switch to larger needles.

Note: You'll now shape the yoke, beginning by working increases at the Front and Back only, then working increases at the Sleeves only, then finally working increases at the Front, Back and Sleeves at the same time. Begin increases for the Front and Back as foll:

Round 1 (Inc, A): *K to marker, SM, brkyobrk, [sl1yo, brk1] to last 2 sts before marker, sl1yo, brkyobrk, SM; rep from * once more. *8 sts inc*

Round 1 (B): *P to marker, SM, sl1yo, p1, [sl1yo, brp1] to 3 sts before marker, sl1yo, p1, sl1yo, SM; rep from * once more.

Luna
by **Anna Strandberg**

Round 2 (A): *K to marker, SM, [brk1, sl1yo] to last st before marker, brk1, SM; rep from * once more.
Round 2 (B): *P to marker, SM, [sl1yo, brp1] to last st before marker, sl1yo, SM; rep from * once more.
Rep rounds 1-2 a further 3 (4, 5, 6, 8) more times. *132 (138, 154, 166, 186) sts*

Begin increasing for Sleeves as foll:
Round 1 (Inc, A): *K1, inv-R, k to last st before marker, inv-L, k1, SM, [brk1, sl1yo] to last st before marker, brk1, SM; rep from * once more. *4 sts inc*
Round 1 (B): *P to marker, SM, [sl1yo, brp1] to last st before marker, sl1yo, SM; rep from * once more.
Round 2 (A): *K to marker, SM, [brk1, sl1yo] to last st before marker, brk1, SM; rep from * once more.
Round 2 (B): *P to marker, SM, [sl1yo, brp1] to last st before marker, sl1yo, SM; rep from * once more.
Rep rounds 1-2 a further 4 (5, 5, 8, 12) times. *152 (162, 178, 202, 238) sts*

Continue to work increases for the Sleeves, Front and Back at the same time:
Round 1 (Inc, A): *K1, inv-R, k to last st, inv-L, k1, SM, brkyobrk, [sl1yo, brk1] to 2 sts before marker, sl1yo, brkyobrk; rep from * once more. *12 sts inc*
Round 1 (B): *P to marker, SM, sl1yo, p1 [sl1yo, brp1] to 3 sts before marker, sl1yo, p1, sl1yo, SM; rep from * once more.
Round 2 (A): *K to marker, SM, [brk1, sl1yo] to last st before marker, brk1, SM; rep from * once more.
Round 2 (B): *P to marker, SM, [sl1yo, brp1] to last st before marker, sl1yo, SM; rep from * once more.
Round 3 (Inc, A): *K1, inv-R, k to last st, inv-L, k1, SM, [brk1, sl1yo] to last st before marker, brk1, SM; rep from * once more. *4 sts inc*
Round 3 (B): *P to marker, SM, [sl1yo, brp1] to last st before marker, sl1yo, SM; rep from * once more.
Round 4 (A): *K to marker, SM, [brk1, sl1yo] to last st before marker, brk1, SM; rep from * once more.
Round 4 (B): *P to marker, SM, [sl1yo, brp1] to last st before marker, sl1yo, SM; rep from * once more.
Rep rounds 1-4 a further 3 (4, 4, 5, 5) times, then rounds 1-3 only once more, ending with a yarn B round. *232 (258, 274, 314, 350) sts*

DIVIDE FOR SLEEVES
Next round (A): Remove marker, place next 47 (50, 52, 62, 72) sts on holder for Right Sleeve, using the backwards loop method cast on 5 (5, 5, 5, 7) sts, PM for new beg of round, cast on 4 (4, 6, 6, 6) sts, remove marker, [brk1, sl1yo] to 1 st before marker, brk1, remove marker, place next 47 (50, 52, 62, 72) sts on holder for Left Sleeve, cast

on 4 (4, 6, 6, 6) sts, PM, cast on 5 (5, 5, 5, 7) sts, remove marker, [brk1, sl1yo] to 6 (6, 6, 6, 8) sts before beg of round marker, brk1.
Shift both strands of yarns across to new beg of round marker as foll:
Arrange both yarn strands on finger, yarn A to the left and yarn B to the right. Always start with yarn A, and follow with yarn B.
Sizes 1, 2, 3 and 4 ONLY: [With yarn A sl1yo, sl st and yo back to LH needle, with yarn B brp1, with yarn A k1, sl st back to LH needle, sl1yo] twice, with yarn A sl1yo, sl st and yo back to LH needle, with yarn B brp1. *5 sts worked*
Size 5 ONLY: [With yarn A sl1yo, sl st and yo back to LH needle, with yarn B brp1, with yarn A k1, sl st back to LH needle, sl1yo] 3 times, with yarn A, sl1yo, sl st and yo back to LH needle, with yarn B brp1. *7 sts worked*

Now continue as foll:
Next round (B): [Sl1yo, p1] 2 (2, 3, 3, 3) times, [sl1yo, brp1] across to 9 (9, 11, 11, 13) cast-on underarm sts, slipping the marker as you pass it, [p1, sl1yo] 4 (4, 5, 5, 6) times across cast-on underarm sts, p1, [brp1, sl1yo] to end. *156 (176, 192, 212, 232) sts; 77 (87, 97, 107, 115) sts for Front, 79 (89, 95, 105, 117) sts for Back*

LOWER BODY
Round 1(A): [Sl1yo, brk1] to end.
Round 1(B): [Brp, sl1yo] to end.
Rep round 1 (A and B) until piece measures 23 (25, 25, 28, 33) cm / 9 (9¾, 9¾, 11, 13)" from underarm or 7 cm / 2¾" less than desired front length, ending with a yarn B round

Front Hem
Row 1 (RS, A): [Sl1yo, brk1] to 1 st before marker, sl1yo, remove marker, place all rem sts on holder for Back, removing beg of round marker. Do not turn, slide Front sts to other end of needle. *77 (87, 97, 107, 115) sts*
Row 1 (RS, B): Brp1, [sl1yo, brp1] to end. Turn work.
Row 2 (WS, A): Sl1yo, [brp1, sl1yo] to end. Slide sts.
Row 2 (WS, B): Brk1, [sl1yo, brk1] to end. Turn work.
Row 3 (RS, A): Sl1yo, [brk1, sl1yo] to end. Slide sts.
Row 3 (RS, B): Brp1, [sl1yo, brp1] to end. Turn work.
Repeat rows 2-3 a further 8 more times, then row 2 only once more, ending with a yarn B WS row.
Break yarn A. With yarn B, cast off using Elastic Cast Off.

Back Hem
With RS facing, return to 79 (89, 95, 105, 117) held Back sts. Join yarns A and B as necessary.
Row 1 (RS, A): K2tog, [sl1yo, brk1] to last 3 sts, sl1yo, ssk. Slide sts. *77 (87, 97, 107, 115) sts*
Row 1 (RS, B): [Sl1yo, brp1] to last st, sl1yo. Turn work.

Luna
by Anna Strandberg

Row 2 (WS, A): Brp1, [sl1yo, brp1] to end. Slide sts.
Row 2 (WS, B): Sl1yo, [brk1, sl1yo] to end. Turn work.
Row 3 (RS, A): Brk1, [sl1yo, brk1] to end. Slide sts.
Row 3 (RS, B): Sl1yo, [brp1, sl1yo] to end. Turn work.
Rep rows 2-3 a further 13 times, then row 2 only once more, ending with a yarn B WS row.
Break yarn A. With yarn B, cast off using Elastic Cast Off.

SLEEVES
Return held Sleeve sts to working needles. Beg at RH corner of underarm cast-on, with yarn B, pick up and knit 5 (5, 7, 7, 7) sts to centre of underarm cast-on, PM to indicate beg of round, pick up and knit 6 (6, 6, 6, 8) sts in rem underarm cast-on. Break yarn B. Slip last 6 (6, 6, 6, 8) sts worked back to LH needle. *58 (61, 65, 75, 87) sts*
Round 1: Join yarn A, sl1, k4, ssk, k to last 7 sts, k2tog, k5. *2 sts dec*
Round 2: Join yarn B, k1, p to last st, sl1.
Round 3: With yarn A, sl1, k to end.
Round 4: With yarn B, k1, p to last st, sl1.
Last two rounds set Striped Garter st pattern.
Continue straight in patt as set for a further 18 (14, 10, 10, 10) rounds.
Dec round: With yarn A, sl1, ssk, k to last 3 sts, k2tog, k1. *2 sts dec*

Working in Striped Garter st pattern throughout, rep Dec round every 20th (18th, 16th, 16th, 16th) round a further 4 (5, 6, 10, 11) times. *48 (49, 51, 53, 61) sts*

Work straight in pattern until sleeve measures 37 (37, 37, 37, 39) cm / 14¼ (14¼, 14¼, 14¼, 15)" from underarm, or 3 cm / 1½" shorter than desired length.
Change to smaller needles. Work in pattern for a further 3 cm / 1½", ending with a yarn B round. Break yarn A. With yarn B, cast off using Elastic Cast Off.

FINISHING
Weave in ends and block to measurements.

a. Bust circumference: 92 (103.5, 113, 124.5, 136.5) cm / 36¼ (40¾, 44½, 49, 53¾)"
b. Neck circumference 54 (54, 58, 60.5, 62) cm / 21¼ (21¼, 22¾, 23¾, 24½)"
c. Length (hem to underarm): 30 (32, 32, 35, 40) cm / 11¾ (12½, 12½, 13¾, 15¾)"
d. Sleeve length: 40 (40, 40, 40, 42) cm / 15¾ (15¾, 15¾, 15¾, 16½)"
e. Upper arm circumference: 26.5 (27, 29.5, 33.5, 38.5) cm / 10½ (11, 11¾, 13¼, 15¼)"
f. Yoke depth: 19 (22, 23, 27, 31) cm / 7½ (8½, 9, 10½, 12¼)"

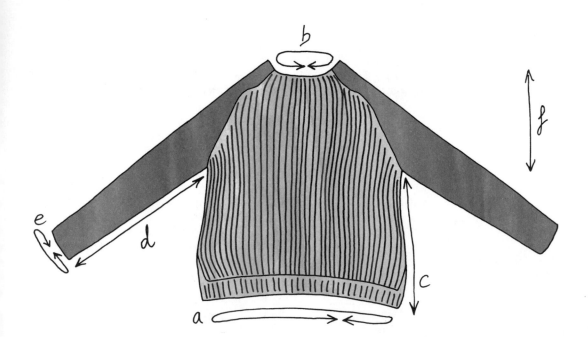

Artemis
by **Esther Romo**

Model has 91 cm / 36" bust, stands 175 cm / 5'9" tall and is wearing a size 2.

Yarn A: Shibui Knits Cima (lace weight; 70% Superbaby Alpaca, 30% Fine Merino; 300 m / 328 yds per 50 g ball)
Shade: Suit; 4 (4, 5, 5, 6) skeins

Yarn B: Shibui Knits Silk Cloud (lace weight; 60% Kid Mohair, 40% Silk; 300 m / 330 yds per 25 g ball)
Shade: Tar; 4 (4, 5, 5, 6) skeins

Yarn C: Anchor Artiste Metallic (4ply/Fingering weight; 80% Viscose, 20% Metallised polyester; 100 m / 109 yds per 25 g ball)
Shade: Gold; 1 skein

Gauge: 28 sts & 38 rows = 10 cm / 4" over Stocking stitch on 3.5 mm needles, with 1 strand each of yarns A and B held together after blocking

Needles: 3.5 mm / US 4 circular needle, 80cm / 32" length
2.75 mm / US 2 circular needle, 80cm / 32" length **AND** needles suitable for working small circumferences in the round.

Always use a needle size that will result in the correct gauge after blocking.

Notions: 4 locking stitch markers, stitch holders or scrap yarn, tapestry needle

Notes: Artemis is knitted from the top down with yarns A and B held together. First the shoulders are knitted separately to create the shape of the front neck, and then the back is worked before joining the body in one piece. The sleeves are knitted in the round from the armholes down. The neck is shaped with short rows to create the special crescent effect.

Stitch Glossary

KRL Knit Through Right Loop: With RH needle, pick up right leg of the stitch below the next stitch on LH needle from back to front and place onto LH needle. Knit this new stitch, then knit the original stitch. *1 st inc*

KLL Knit Through Left Loop: With LH needle, pick up left leg of stitch 2 rows below stitch just worked on RH needle from back to front. Knit this new stitch through the back loop. *1 st inc*

PRL Purl Through Right Loop: With LH needle, pick up purl bump 2 rows below the stitch just worked on RH needle from bottom to top. Purl this new stitch. *1 st inc*

PLL Purl Through Left Loop: With RH needle, pick up purl bump of the stitch below the next stitch on LH needle and place onto LH needle without twisting. Purl this new stitch through the back loop, then purl the original stitch. *1 st inc*

Kwtog: Pick up the wrap of the next st with the RH needle, place it on the LH needle and knit the wrap tog with its st.

Pwtog: Pick up the wrap of the next st with the RH needle, place it on the LH needle and purl the wrap tog with its st.

Sizes: 1 (2, 3, 4, 5)
Finished bust circumference: 99 (109, 121, 129, 141) cm / 39 (43, 48, 51¾, 55½)" – to be worn with 10 - 20 cm / 4 - 8" positive ease

Artemis
by Esther Romo

PATTERN BEGINS
Note: Yarns A and B are held together throughout.

LEFT SHOULDER
** Using larger needles, yarns A and B held together and the long-tail method, cast on 8 sts.
Set-up row (WS): P3, PM, p2, PM, p3.
Row 1 (RS): K to 1 st before marker, KRL, SM, k2, SM, KLL, k to end. *2 sts inc*
Row 2 (WS): P to 1 st before marker, PRL, SM, p2, SM, PLL, p to end. *2 sts inc*
Rows 3-20: Rep rows 1-2 a further 9 times. *48 sts **
Next row (RS): K1, M1L, k to 1 st before marker, KRL, SM, k2, SM, KLL, k to end. *3 sts inc*
Next row (WS): P to 1 st before marker, PRL, SM, p2, SM, PLL, p to end. *2 sts inc*
Rep last two rows a further 6 (8, 9, 9, 10) times. *83 (93, 98, 98, 103) sts*
Next row (RS): Using the cable method, cast on 2 sts, k to 1 st before marker, KRL, SM, k2, SM, KLL, k to end. *4 sts inc*
Next row (WS): P to 1 st before marker, PRL, SM, p2, SM, PLL, p to end. *2 sts inc*
Rep last two rows once more. *95 (105, 110, 110, 115) sts*
Next row (RS): Using the cable method, cast on 3 sts, k to 1 st before marker, KRL, SM, k2, SM, KLL, k to end. *5 sts inc*
Next row (WS): P to 1 st before marker, PRL, SM, p2, SM, PLL, p to end. *2 sts inc*
Rep last two rows once more. *109 (119, 124, 124, 129) sts 62 (68, 71, 71, 74) sts on neck side, 2 seam sts, 45 (49, 51, 51, 53) sts on armhole side*
Place sts on hold.

RIGHT SHOULDER
Work as for Left Shoulder from ** to **.
Next row (RS): K to 1 st before marker, KRL, SM, k2, SM, KLL, k to last st, M1R, k1. *3 sts inc*
Next row (WS): P to 1 st before marker, PRL, SM, p2, SM, PLL, p to end. *2 sts inc*
Rep last two rows a further 6 (8, 9, 9, 10) times. *83 (93, 98, 98, 103) sts*
Next row (RS): K to 1 st before marker, KRL, SM, k2, SM, KLL, k to end. *2 sts inc*
Next row (WS): Using the cable method, cast on 2 sts, p to 1 st before marker, PRL, SM, p2, SM, PLL, p to end. *4 sts inc*
Rep last two rows once more. *95 (105, 110, 110, 115) sts*
Next row (RS): K to 1 st before marker, KRL, SM, k2, SM, KLL, k to end. *2 sts inc*

Next row (WS): Using the cable method, cast on 3 sts, p to 1 st before marker, PRL, SM, p2, SM, PLL, p to end. *5 sts inc*
Rep last two rows once more. *109 (119, 124, 124, 129) sts 62 (68, 71, 71, 74) sts on neck side, 2 seam sts, 45 (49, 51, 51, 53) sts on armhole side*

FRONT
Sizes 1 & 2 ONLY
Set-up row (RS): K to marker, SM, k2, SM, k to end of Right Shoulder, turn work, using cable method cast on 9 (10, -, -, -) sts, turn work. With RS facing knit across 62 (68, -, -, -) held Left Shoulder sts to marker, remove marker, slip rem 47 (51, -, -,) sts to holder for Back Shoulder, turn work.
Next row (WS): P to marker, remove marker, slip rem 47 (51, -, -, -) sts to holder for Back Shoulder, turn work. *133 (146, -, -, -) sts*
Work in St st across Front sts for a further 59 (61, -, -, -) rows, ending with a RS row.

Sizes 3, 4 & 5 ONLY
Set-up row (RS): K to 1 st before marker, KRL, SM, k2, SM, KLL, k to end of Right Shoulder, turn work, using cable method cast on - (-, 12, 14, 16) sts, turn work. With RS facing knit across held Left shoulder sts to marker, KRL, SM, k2, SM, KLL, k to end. *- (-, 264, 266, 278) sts.*
Row 1 (WS): [P to 1 st before marker, PRL, SM, p2, SM, PLL] twice, p to end. *4 sts inc*
Row 2 (RS): [K to 1 st before next marker, KRL, SM, k2, SM, KLL] twice, k to end. *4 sts inc*
Rep rows 1-2 a further - (-, 1, 3, 5) times. *- (-, 280, 298, 326) sts.*
Next row (WS): P to marker, SM, p2, SM, p to marker, remove marker, slip rem - (-, 58, 62, 68) sts to holder for Back Shoulder, turn work.
Next row (RS): K to marker, remove marker, slip rem - (-, 58, 62, 68) sts to holder for Back Shoulder, turn work. *- (-, 164, 174, 190) sts*
Work in St st across Front sts for - (-, 64, 68, 72) rows, ending with a RS row.

ALL sizes again
Break yarn and place all Front sts on hold.

RIGHT BACK SHOULDER
With RS facing, return to held Right Shoulder sts and rejoin yarn, leaving last 2 sts on hold and removing marker. *45 (49, 56, 60, 66) sts*
Row 1 (RS): Knit.

Artemis
by Esther Romo

Row 2 (WS): Purl.
Rep rows 1-2 a further 29 (30, 32, 33, 33) times.
Next row (RS): K1, M1L, k to end. *1 st inc*
Next row (WS): Purl.
Rep last two rows a further 6 (8, 9, 9, 10) times. *52 (58, 66, 70, 77) sts*
Next row (RS): Using the cable method, cast on 2 sts, k to end. *2 sts inc*
Next row (WS): Purl.
Rep last two rows once more. *56 (62, 70, 74, 81) sts*
Next row (RS): Using the cable method, cast on 3 sts, k to end. *3 sts inc*
Next row (WS): Purl.
Rep last two rows once more. **62 (68, 76, 80, 87) sts**
Break yarn and place sts on hold.

LEFT BACK SHOULDER
With RS facing, return to held Left Shoulder sts and rejoin yarn, leaving first 2 sts on hold and removing marker. *45 (49, 56, 60, 66) sts*
Row 1 (RS): Knit.
Row 2 (WS): Purl.
Rep rows 1-2 a further 29 (30, 32, 33, 33) times.
Next row (RS): K to last st, M1R, k1. *1 st inc*
Next row (WS): Purl.
Rep last two rows a further 6 (8, 9, 9, 10) times. *52 (58, 66, 70, 77) sts*
Next row (RS): Knit.
Next row (WS): Using the cable method, cast on 2 sts, p to end. *2 sts inc*
Rep last two rows once more. *56 (62, 70, 74, 81) sts*
Next row (RS): Knit.
Next row (WS): Using the cable method, cast on 3 sts, p to end. *3 sts inc*
Rep last two rows once more. *62 (68, 76, 80, 87) sts.*
Do not break yarn.

BODY
Set-up row (RS): K to end of Left Back Shoulder sts, turn work, using the cable method cast on 9 (10, 12, 14, 16) sts, turn work, k to end of held Right Back Shoulder sts, turn work, using the cable method cast on 4 sts, turn work, k to end of held Front sts, turn work, using the cable method cast on 4 sts, turn work, join to work in the round and PM to indicate beg of round. *274 (300, 336, 356, 388) sts*
Work St st in the round for 98 (100, 104, 110, 116) rounds.
Change to smaller needles. Knit 1 round and evenly increase 22 (24, 26, 28, 30) sts. *296 (324, 362, 384, 418) sts*
Rib round: [K1, p1] to end.
Rep Rib round for a further 17 rounds.
Cast off all sts loosely.

SLEEVES
Using larger needles suitable for working small circumferences in the round and yarns A and B held together, beg at centre of underarm cast-on sts, pick up and k39 (41, 44, 46, 48) sts up one side of armhole to shoulder, knit across 2 held shoulder sts, pick up and k39 (41, 44, 46, 48) sts down other side of armhole, join to work in the round and PM to indicate beg of round. *80 (84, 90, 94, 98) sts*
Work in St st for 21 rounds.

Dec round: K1, ssk, k to 3 sts before marker, k2tog, k1. *2 sts dec*
Continue in St st and rep Dec round every foll 6th round a further 9 (10, 10, 12, 14) times. *60 (62, 68, 68, 68) sts*
Work straight in St st until sleeve measures 35 (35, 35, 36, 36) cm / 13¾ (13¾, 13¾, 14, 14)" from underarm.

Change to smaller needles.
Rib round: [K1, p1] to end.
Rep Rib round for a further 14 rounds. Break yarns A and B.
Change to yarn C.
Rep Rib round for a further 4 rounds.
Cast off all sts loosely.

NECKLACE HALF MOON
Using smaller needles and yarn C, beg at centre of back neck, pick up sts as foll: Pick up and knit 1 st, PM, pick up and knit 239 (243, 255, 259, 269) sts evenly around neckline, join to work in the round and PM to indicate beg of round. *240 (244, 256, 260, 270) sts.*

Artemis

by Esther Romo

Short row 1 (RS): K1, SM, [p1, k1] 7 times, p1, sl1 wyif, w&t.

Short row 2 (WS): Sl1 wyif, [k1, p1] 7 times, k1, SM, p1, SM, [k1, p1] 7 times, k1, sl1 wyif, w&t.

Short row 3: Sl1 wyif, [p1, k1] 7 times, p1, SM, k1, SM, [p1, k1] 7 times, p1, kwtog, [p1, k1] 3 times, sl1 wyif, w&t.

Short row 4: Sl1 wyif, [p1, k1] 11 times, SM, p1, SM, [k1, p1] 7 times, p1, pwtog, [p1, k1] 3 times, sl1 wyif, w&t.

Short row 5: Sl1 wyif, [k1, p1] 11 times, SM, k1, SM, [p1, k1] 11 times, kwtog, [p1, k1] 3 times, sl1 wyif, w&t.

Short row 6: Sl1 wyif, [k1, p1] 14 times, k1, SM, p1, SM, [k1, p1] 11 times, kwtog, [p1, k1] 3 times, sl1 wyif, w&t.

Short row 7: Sl1 wyif, [p1, k1] 14 times, p1, SM, k1, SM, [p1, k1] 14 times, p1, kwtog, [p1, k1] 3 times, sl1 wyif, w&t.

Short row 8: Sl1 wyif, [p1, k1] 18 times, SM, p1, SM, [k1, p1] 14 times, pwtog, [p1, k1] 3 times, sl1 wyif, w&t.

Short row 9: Sl1 wyif, [k1, p1] 18 times, SM, k1, SM, [p1, k1] 18 times, pwtog, [p1, k1] 3 times, sl1 wyif, w&t.

Short row 10: Sl1 wyif, [k1, p1] 21 times, k1, SM, p1, SM, [k1, p1] 18 times, kwtog, [p1, k1] 3 times, sl1 wyif, w&t.

Short row 11: Sl1 wyif, [p1, k1] 21 times, p1, SM, k1, SM, [p1, k1] 21 times, p1, kwtog, [p1, k1] 3 times, sl1 wyif, w&t.

Short row 12: Sl1 wyif, [p1, k1] 25 times, SM, p1, SM, [k1, p1] 21 times, k1, pwtog, [p1, k1] 3 times, sl1 wyif, w&t.

Short row 13: Sl1 wyif, [k1, p1] 25 times, SM, k1, SM, [p1, k1] 25 times, p1, pwtog, [p1, k1] 3 times, sl1 wyif, w&t.

Short row 14: Sl1 wyif, [k1, p1] 28 times, k1, SM, p1, SM, [k1, p1] 25 times, kwtog, [p1, k1] 3 times, sl1 wyif, PM to indicate new beg of round, w&t.

Short row 15: Sl1 wyif, [k1, p1] 28 times, p1, remove marker, k1, remove marker, [p1, k1] 28 times, p1, kwtog, [p1, k1] to marker.

Round 1: Pwtog, [k1, p1] to marker.

Round 2: [K1, p1] to end.

Rep round 2 for a further 6 rounds.

Cast off all sts loosely.

FINISHING

Weave in ends and block to measurements.

a. Bust circumference: 99 (109, 121, 129, 141) cm / 39 (43, 48, 51¾, 55½)"

b. Length (underarm to hem): 28.5 (29, 30, 31.5, 33) cm / 11¼ (11½, 11¾, 12¼, 13)"

c. Sleeve length: 41 (41, 41, 42, 42) cm / 16¼ (16¼, 16¼, 16½, 16½)"

d. Upper arm circumference: 29 (30, 32, 33.5, 35) cm / 11½ (11¾, 12½, 13¼, 13¾)"

e. Wrist circumference: 17.5 (18, 19.5, 19.5, 19.5) cm / 6¾ (7, 7½, 7½, 7½,)"

f: Neck width: 19.5 (20, 22, 23, 24) cm / 7½ (8, 8¾, 9, 9½)"

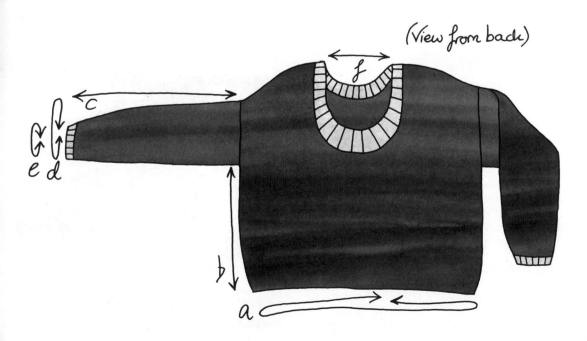

(View from back)

Hecate
by Maddie Harvey

One Size: 170 cm / 67" long x 44 cm / 17½" wide
Yarn A: Woollenflower Masgot Fine (4ply/Fingering; 100% wool; 200 m / 218 yds per 50 g skein)
Shade: Indigo dyed; 3 skeins
Yarn B: Woollenflower Whorl (lace weight; 72% fine kid mohair, 28% silk; 420 m / 459 yds per 50 g skein)
Shade: Avocado dyed; 1 skein
Gauge: 17 sts & 28.5 rows = 10 cm / 4" over main pattern on 4.5 mm needles after blocking.
Needles: 4.5 mm / US 7 circular needle, 60 cm / 24" length AND one spare straight needle in the same size.
Always use a needle size that will result in the correct gauge after blocking.
Notions: 6 locking stitch markers, 3 stitch markers, additional spare 4.5 mm straight needle (optional, for 3-needle cast-off), tapestry needle
Notes: Hecate is a parallelogram-shaped wrap, worked in two pieces towards the centre, and joined in the middle with a 3-needle cast off. Each piece begins with an i-cord tab and increases at one edge to make the points of the parallelogram, and then worked without increases to create the centre of the wrap.
The moon motifs are worked in stripes of yarn B, which can be loosely carried up the i-cord by twisting the yarns together at the beginning of every RS row. Work the i-cord edge stitches as loosely as possible.
After both pieces are joined together, stitches are picked up along the two long edges and the edging is worked in yarn B. Work the edging stitches as loosely as possible. The cast off includes bobbles, worked every two charted pattern repeats, to line up with the moon motifs.

Stitch Glossary
Catch Strands: Insert RH needle under the 2 strands of yarn B below and knit them with the next stitch, catching the strands.
MB (make bobble): [(K2tog tbl, yo) twice, k2tog tbl] into next 2 sts, turn, p5, turn, kfb 5 times, lift 9 sts over the top st, and off the needle.

Chart A Written Instructions
Row 1 (RS): Using yarn A, k3, yo, k to end. *1 st inc*
Row 2 (WS): Sl3 wyif, p to last 4 sts, p1tbl, sl3 wyif.
Row 3: Using yarn B, k3, yo, k1, [sl3 wyif, p3] to last 6 sts, sl3 wyif, k3. *1 st inc*
Row 4: Sl3 wyif, sl3 wyib, [k3, sl3 wyib] to last 5 sts, p1, p1tbl, sl3 wyif.
Rows 5-6: Rep rows 1-2.
Row 7: K3, yo, k3, [k1, catch strands, k4] to last 6 sts, k1, catch strands, k4. *1 st inc*
Row 8: Sl3 wyif, k to last 4 sts, k1tbl, sl3 wyif.
Row 9: K3, yo, k to end. *1 st inc*

Row 10: Sl3 wyif, k to last 4 sts, k1tbl, sl3 wyif.
Rows 11-12: Rep rows 9-10 once more. *1 st inc*

Chart B Written Instructions
Row 1 (RS): Using yarn A, knit.
Row 2 (WS): Sl3 wyif, p to last 3 sts, sl3 wyif.
Row 3: Using yarn B, k3, [sl3 wyif, p3] to last 6 sts, sl3 wyif, k3.
Row 4: Sl3 wyif, sl3 wyib, [k3, sl3 wyib] to last 3 sts, sl3 wyif.
Rows 5-6: Rep rows 1-2 once more.
Row 7: K3, [k1, catch strands, k4] to end.
Row 8: Sl3 wyif, k to last 3 sts, sl3 wyif.
Row 9: Knit.
Row 10: Sl3 wyif, k to last 3 sts, sl3 wyif.
Rows 11-12: Rep rows 9-10 once more.

PATTERN BEGINS
LEFT SIDE
** Using the long-tail method and yarn A, cast on 3 sts.
Next Row: K3, sl3 wyif back to LH needle, do not turn. Rep last row a further 3 times.
Next Row (RS): K3, turn work 90 degrees clockwise, miss the next i-cord st, pick up 1 st, yo, miss the next i-cord st, pick up 1 st, miss the next i-cord st, turn work 90 degrees clockwise, pick up 3 sts along cast-on edge. *9 sts*
Next Row (WS): Sl3 wyif, p3, sl3 wyif.

Hecate
by Maddie Harvey

Set-Up

Row 1 (RS): K3, yo, k to end. *10 sts*

Row 2 (WS): Sl3 wyif, p to last 4 sts, p1tbl, sl3 wyif.

Rows 3-6: Rep rows 1-2 twice. *12 sts*

Row 7: K3, yo, k to end. *13 sts*

Row 8: Sl3 wyif, k to last 4 sts, k1tbl, sl3 wyif.

Rows 9-12: Rep rows 7-8 twice. *15 sts*

With RS facing, mark the i-cord edge on the LH side with a locking stitch marker.

Following the chart or written instructions, work from Chart A until rows 1-12 have been worked a total of 10 times. *75 sts*

With RS facing, mark the i-cord edge st on the RH side with a locking stitch marker.

Following the chart or written instructions, work from Chart B until rows 1-12 have been worked a total of 12 times.

With RS facing, mark the i-cord edge st on the RH side with a locking stitch marker.

Rep rows 1-2 only of Chart B once more. **

Place sts on spare needle and set aside.

RIGHT SIDE

Work as for Left Side from ** to **.

With RS facing, slide the sts along the circular needle to the LH side.

Join the right side and left side together: With WS together, using the other tip of the circular needle or a spare needle, and yarn B, work a 3-needle cast off across Right and Left Side sts.

Edging

The edging is worked along both long edges of the parallelogram in yarn B.

When picking up stitches along the i-cord edge, there should be six picked-up sts per repeat of rows 1-12 of the chart pattern.

Top Edge

With RS facing, using yarn B and beg at the marked corner (from the last row of Chart A) in the i-cord stitch to the right of the marker, pick up and knit 71 sts to next marker, remove locking stitch marker, pick up and knit 1 st in marked st, PM, pick up and knit 3 sts to 3-needle cast off join, PM, pick up and knit 132 sts to next marker, remove locking stitch marker, PM, pick up and knit 10 sts to corner. *217 sts*

Next Row (WS): Knit.

Rep last row twice more.

Cast off with RS facing as foll:

Set-up: K1, sl st from RH needle to LH needle, MB.

Step 1: [Sl st from RH needle to LH needle, k2tog tbl] eleven times.

Step 2: Sl st from RH needle to LH needle, MB.

Rep steps 1-2 a further 4 times, then rep step 1 only once more.

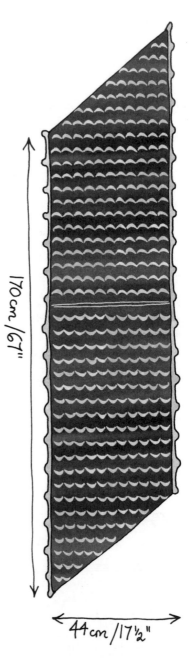

170cm / 67"

44cm / 17½"

Hecate
by **Maddie Harvey**

Next Step: Remove marker, sl st from RH needle to LH needle, MB.

Rep steps 1-2 a further 11 times.

Next Step: Remove marker, sl st from RH needle to LH needle, k2tog tbl, remove marker, [sl st from RH needle to LH needle, k2tog tbl] eight times, sl st from RH needle to LH needle, MB, sl st from RH needle to LH needle, k2tog tbl.

Fasten off.

Bottom Edge

Work as for Top Edge along opposite side.

FINISHING

Weave in ends and block to measurements.

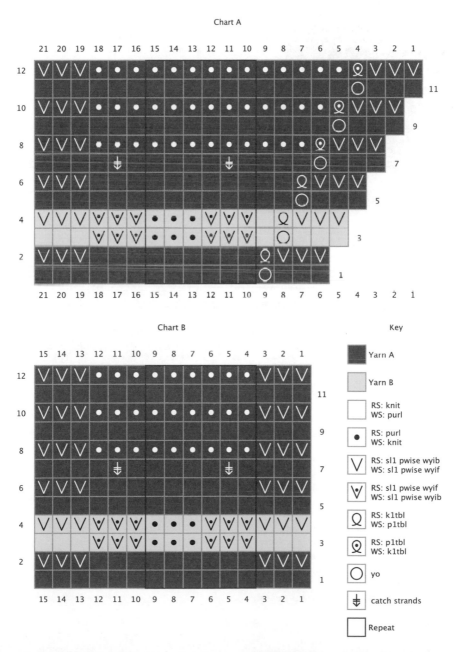

Chart A

Chart B

Key

Yarn A

Yarn B

RS: knit
WS: purl

RS: purl
WS: knit

RS: sl1 pwise wyib
WS: sl1 pwise wyif

RS: sl1 pwise wyif
WS: sl1 pwise wyib

RS: k1tbl
WS: p1tbl

RS: p1tbl
WS: k1tbl

yo

catch strands

Repeat

Ceridwen
by Fiona Alice

Sizes: 1 (2, 3, 4, 5, 6)
Bust circumference: 86.5 (96.5, 106.5, 117, 127, 137) cm / 34 (38, 42, 46, 50, 54)" - to be worn with 10 - 15 cm / 4 - 6" positive ease
Model has 91 cm / 36" bust, stands 173 cm / 5'8" tall and is wearing a size 3.
Yarn: Illimani Yarn Amelie (Aran weight; 56% mulberry silk, 40% baby alpaca, 4% merino wool; 150 m / 164 yds per 50 g skein)
Shade: Charcoal (ZK55); 7 (8, 9, 10, 12, 13) skeins
Gauge: 20 sts & 30 rows = 10 cm / 4" over reverse stocking stitch on 4.5 mm needles after blocking.
24 sts & 30 rows = 10 cm / 4" over Centre Cable Panel (Chart C) on 5 mm needles after blocking.
Needles: 4.5 mm / US 7 knitting needles **AND** circular needle, 40 cm / 16" length
5 mm / US 8 knitting needles
Always use a needle size that will result in the correct gauge after blocking.
Notions: 6 stitch markers, 3 locking stitch markers, cable needle, stitch holder or scrap yarn, tapestry needle
Notes: Ceridwen is worked flat and in the pieces before seaming them together. The neckband is picked up last and folded over for a smooth finish. If working with Illimani's Amelie, be careful not to accidentally push the needle directly through the yarn. If too forceful, this can break the silk core of the yarn.

Stitch Glossary
1/2 RPC: Sl 2 sts to cable needle, hold at back, k1, p2 from cable needle.
1/2 LPC: Sl 1 sts to cable needle, hold at front, p2, k1 from cable needle.
2/2 RPC: Sl 2 sts to cable needle, hold at back, k2, p2 from cable needle.
2/2 LPC: Sl 2 sts to cable needle, hold at front, p2, k2 from cable needle.

Written Instructions for Charts
Chart A (worked over a multiple of 4 sts)
Row 1 (RS): [1/2 RPC, P1] to marker.
Row 2 (WS): [K3, p1] to marker.
Row 3: [K1, p3] to marker.
Row 4: Rep row 2.
Row 5: [1/2 LPC, p1] to marker.
Row 6: [K1, p1, k2] to marker.
Row 7: [P2, k1, p1] to marker.
Row 8: Rep row 6.

Chart B (worked over a multiple of 5 sts)
Row 1 (RS): [2/2 RPC, P1] to marker.
Row 2 (WS): [K3, p2] to marker.
Row 3: [K2, p3] to marker.
Row 4: Rep row 2.
Row 5: [2/2 LPC, p1] to marker.
Row 6: [K1, p2, k2] to marker.
Row 7: [P2, k2, p1] to marker.
Row 8: Rep row 6.

Chart C (worked over a multiple of 8 sts)
Row 1 (RS): [2/2 RPC, 2/2 LPC] to marker.
Row 2 (WS): [P2, k4, p2] to marker.
Row 3: [K2, p4, k2] to marker.
Row 4: Rep row 2.
Row 5: [2/2 LPC, 2/2 RPC] to marker.
Row 6: [K2, p4, k2] to marker.
Row 7: [P2, k4, p2] to marker.
Row 8: Rep row 6.

Chart D (worked over a multiple of 5 sts)
Row 1 (RS): [P1, 2/2 LPC] to marker.
Row 2 (WS): [P2, k3] to marker.
Row 3: [P3, k2] to marker.
Row 4: Rep row 2.
Row 5: [P1, 2/2 RPC] to marker.
Row 6: [K2, p2, k1] to marker.
Row 7: [P1, k2, p2] to marker.
Row 8: Rep row 6.

Ceridwen
by Fiona Alice

Chart E (worked over a multiple of 4 sts)
Row 1 (RS): [P1, 1/2 LPC] to marker.
Row 2 (WS): [P1, k3] to marker.
Row 3: [P3, k1] to marker.
Row 4: Rep row 2.
Row 5: [P1, 1/2 RPC] to marker.
Row 6: [K2, p1, k1] to marker.
Row 7: [P1, k1, p2] to marker.
Row 8: Rep row 6.

Chart F (worked over a multiple of 4 sts plus 2)
Row 1: P1, [p1, 1/2 LPC] to last st, p1.
Row 2: K1, [p1, k3] to last st, k1.
Row 3: P1, [p3, k1] to last st, p1.
Row 4: Rep row 2.
Row 5: P1, [p1, 2/1 RPC] to last st, p1.
Row 6: K1, [k2, p1, k1] to last st, k1.
Row 7: P1, [p1, k1, p2] to last st, p1.
Row 8: Rep row 6.

Chart G (worked over a multiple of 4 sts plus 2)
Row 1: P1, [2/1 RPC, p1] to last st, p1.
Row 2: K1, [k3, p1] to last st, k1.
Row 3: P1, [k1, p3] to last st, p1.
Row 4: Rep row 2.
Row 5: P1, [1/2 LPC, p1] to last st, p1.
Row 6: K1, [k1, p1, k2] to last st, k1.
Row 7: P1, [p2, k1, p1] to last st, p1.
Row 8: Rep row 6.

PATTERN BEGINS
FRONT
** Using larger needles and the long-tail method, cast on
10 (10, 12, 12, 9, 11) sts, PM, cast on 16 (16, 20, 20, 24, 24)
sts, PM, cast on 15 (20, 20, 25, 25, 30) sts, PM, cast on 24
(24, 24, 24, 32, 32) sts, PM, cast on 15 (20, 20, 25, 25, 30)
sts, PM, cast on 16 (16, 20, 20, 24, 24), PM, cast on 10
(10, 12, 12, 9, 11) sts. *106 (116, 128, 138, 148, 162) sts*
Set-up row (WS): K to marker, SM, [k2, p1, k1] to marker,
SM, [k2, p2, k1] to marker, SM, [k2, p4, k2] to marker,
SM, [k1, p2, k2] to marker, SM, [k1, p1, k2] to marker,
SM, k to end.
Following charts or written instructions, establish Charts
as foll:
Row 1 (RS): P to marker, SM, work row 1 of Chart A to
marker, SM, work row 1 of Chart B to marker, SM, work
row 1 of Chart C to marker, SM, work row 1 of Chart D to
marker, SM, work row 1 of Chart E to marker, SM, p to end.
Row 2 (WS): K to marker, SM, work next row of Chart E
to marker, SM, work next row of Chart D to marker, SM,
work next row of Chart C to marker, SM, work next row
of Chart B to marker, SM, work next row of Chart A to

marker, SM, k to end.
Last two rows set patt. Continue as set, working next row
of Charts each time, until piece measures 7.5 cm / 3",
ending with a WS row.
Dec Row (RS): P1, p2tog, patt to last 3 sts, ssp, p1. *2 sts dec*
Work straight in patt for 17 (17, 19, 19, 21, 21) rows.
Rep last 18 (18, 20, 20, 22, 22) rows a further 4 times. *96
(106, 118, 128, 138, 152) sts ***
Work straight in patt until Front measures 52 (53.5, 56,
59.5, 61.5, 63) cm / 20½ (21, 22, 23½, 24¼, 24¾)" from
cast-on edge, ending with a WS row.
Keeping established patt correct throughout, shape
shoulders as foll, removing markers as necessary:
Set-up Row (RS): Patt across 40 (45, 50, 54, 59, 65) sts for
Left Shoulder, cast off next 16 (16, 18, 20, 20, 22) sts, patt
to end. *40 (45, 50, 54, 59, 65) sts*
Work each shoulder separately. Place Left Shoulder sts on
hold and continue on Right Shoulder sts only.

Right Shoulder
Row 1 (WS): Patt to end.
Row 2: Cast off 3 sts, patt to end. *37 (42, 47, 51, 56, 62) sts*
Row 3: Patt to end.
Row 4: Cast off 2 sts, patt to end. *35 (40, 45, 49, 54, 60) sts*
Rows 5-6: Rep rows 3-4. *33 (38, 43, 47, 52, 58) sts*
Row 7: Patt to end.
Row 8: Dec 1 st (working as k2tog or p2tog as required to
keep the pattern correct), patt to end. *1 st dec*
Rep rows 7-8 a further 4 (4, 4, 4, 5, 5) times. *28 (33, 38, 42,
46, 52) sts*
Work straight in patt until Front measures 61 (62, 65, 66,
68.5, 70) cm / 24 (24½, 25½, 26, 27, 27½)" from cast-on
edge, ending with a WS row. Place Right Shoulder sts on
hold and break yarn, leaving a long tail for 3-needle
cast off.

Left Shoulder
With WS facing, rejoin yarn to held Left Shoulder sts.
Row 1 (WS): Cast off 3 sts, patt to end. *37 (42, 47, 51, 56,
62) sts*
Row 2: Patt to end.
Row 3: Cast off 2 sts, patt to end. *35 (40, 45, 49, 54, 60) sts*
Rows 4-5: Rep rows 2-3. *33 (38, 43, 47, 52, 58) sts*
Row 6: Patt to end.
Row 7: Dec 1 st (working as ssk or ssp as required to keep
the pattern correct), patt to end. *1 st dec*
Rep rows 6-7 a further 4 (4, 4, 4, 5, 5) times. *28 (33, 38,
42, 46, 52) sts*
Work straight in pattern until Front measures 61 (62, 65, 66,
68.5, 70) cm / 24 (24½, 25½, 26, 27, 27½)" from cast-on
edge, ending with a WS row. Place Left Shoulder sts on
hold and break yarn, leaving a long tail for 3-needle cast off.

Ceridwen
by **Fiona Alice**

BACK

Work as for Front from ** to **.

Work straight in patt until Back measures 58.5 (59.5, 62, 63.5, 66, 67.5) cm / 23 (23½, 24½, 25, 26, 26½)" from cast-on edge, ending with a WS row.

Keeping established patt correct throughout, shape shoulders as foll, removing markers as necessary:

Set-up row (RS): Patt across 32 (37, 42, 46, 50, 56) sts for Right Shoulder, cast off next 32 (32, 34, 36, 38, 40) sts, patt to end. *32 (37, 42, 46, 50, 56) sts*

Work each shoulder separately. Place Right Shoulder sts on hold and continue on Left Shoulder sts only.

Left Shoulder

Row 1 (WS): Patt to end.
Row 2: Cast off 2 sts, patt to end. *30 (35, 40, 44, 48, 54) sts*
Row 3: Patt to end.
Rows 4-5: Rep rows 2-3. *28 (33, 38, 42, 46, 52) sts*
Row 6: Patt to end.
Break yarn, leaving a tail to weave in later, and place sts on hold.

Right Shoulder

Row 1 (WS): Cast off 2 sts, patt to end. *30 (35, 40, 44, 48, 54) sts*
Row 2: Patt to end.
Rows 3-4: Rep rows 1-2. *28 (33, 38, 42, 46, 52) sts*
Row 5: Patt to end.
Break yarn, leaving a tail to weave in later, and place sts on hold.

SLEEVES

Using smaller needles and the long-tail method, cast on 46 (46, 50, 54, 54, 58) sts.
Follow correct instructions for Left or Right Cuff:

Left Cuff ONLY

Set-up Row (WS): K1, [k2, p1, k1] to last st, k1.
Row 1 (RS): Following Chart or written instructions, work row 1 of Chart F, working 4-st rep 11 (11, 12, 13, 13, 14) times across the row.
Row 2: Work next row of Chart F.
Continue to work through Chart F as set until rows 1-8 have been worked twice in total, then rep rows 1-6 only once more.

Right Cuff ONLY

Set-up Row (WS): K1, [k1, p1, k2] to last st, k1.
Row 1 (RS): Following chart or written instructions, work row 1 of Chart G, working 4-st rep 11 (11, 12, 13, 13, 14) times across the row.
Row 2: Work next row of Chart G.
Continue to work through Chart G as set until rows 1-8 have been worked twice in total, then rep rows 1-6 only once more.

BOTH Sleeves

Work 2 rows in rev St st.
Inc row (RS): P1, M1LP, p to last st, M1RP, p1. *2 sts inc*
Work straight in rev St st for 4 rows.
Inc row (WS): K1, M1R, k to last st, M1L, k1.
Working inc on RS or WS row as set, rep Inc row every 5th row a further 10 (13, 13, 14, 16, 17) times. *70 (76, 80, 86, 90, 96) sts*
Work straight in rev St st until Sleeve measures 43 (45.5, 48.5, 49.5, 51, 52) cm / 17 (18, 19, 19½, 20, 20½)" from cast-on edge, or desired length, ending with a RS row. Cast off.
Note: Sleeve length will also be affected by the drop shoulder, so take this into consideration when deciding sleeve length.
Repeat for second sleeve, working opposite Cuff.

Ceridwen
by **Fiona Alice**

FINISHING

Holding RS together, using the long yarn ends, join Front and Back shoulders with 3-needle cast off.

To attach sleeves, begin by marking the centre of each sleeve with a locking stitch marker. Take two more spare locking stitch markers and mark 18 (19, 20.5, 21.5, 22.5, 24) cm / 7 (7½, 8, 8½, 9, 9½)" down from either side of the shoulder seam. Line the sleeve marker up with the shoulder seam. Sew the sleeve in place, starting at the shoulder seam and working down towards each marker. Sew side seams from hem to underarm using rev St st mattress stitch. Sew sleeve seams from cuff to underarm.

Neckband

Using smaller circular needles, beg at right shoulder seam, pick up and knit 38 (38, 40, 42, 44, 46) sts evenly across Back then pick up and knit 54 (54, 56, 58, 62, 64) sts evenly across Front. Join to work in the round. PM to indicate beg of round. 92 (92, 96, 100, 106, 110) sts

Round 1: Purl.

Round 2: Knit.

Rounds 3-11: Rep round 2.

Break yarn leaving a very long tail. Fold neckband in half to WS and use a tapestry needle and the long tail to sew the live stitches on needle to the corresponding picked up stitch directly below, working around entire neckband.

Finishing

Weave in ends and gently block to measurements. The body of the sweater may need to be stretched out slightly since the cable pattern will naturally pull inwards.

a. Finished bust circumference: 86.5 (96.5, 106.5, 117, 127, 137) cm / 34 (38, 42, 46, 50, 54)"

b. Bottom circumference: 96.5 (106.5, 117, 127, 137, 147.5) cm / 38 (42, 46, 50, 54, 58)"

c. Full length: 61 (62, 65, 66, 68.5, 70) cm / 24 (24½, 25½, 26, 27, 27½)"

d. Side seam length: 43 (43, 44.5, 44.5, 45.5, 45.5) cm / 17 (17, 17½, 17½, 18, 18)"

e. Upper arm circumference: 35.5 (38, 40.5, 43.5, 45.5, 48.5) cm / 14 (15, 16, 17, 18, 19)"

f. Cuff circumference: 19 (19, 20.5, 22, 22, 23.5) cm / 7½ (7½, 8, 8¾, 8¾, 9¼)"

g. Sleeve length: 43 (45.5, 48.5, 49.5, 51, 52) cm / 17 (18, 19, 19½, 20, 20½)"

h. Shoulder width: 12.5 (15.5, 17.5, 20.5, 22.5, 25) cm / 5 (6, 7, 8, 8¾, 9¾)"

i. Neck width: 18 (18, 19, 20.5, 21, 21.5) cm / 7 (7, 7½, 8, 8¼, 8½)"

j. Neckband: 2 cm / ¾"

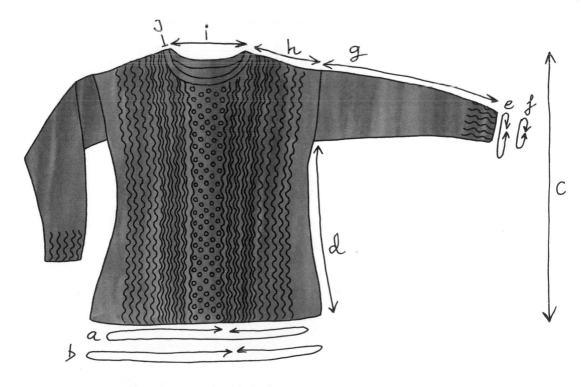

Chart E

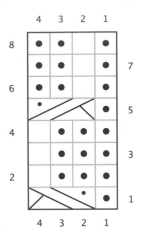

Chart D

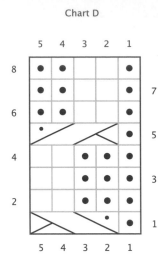

Chart C

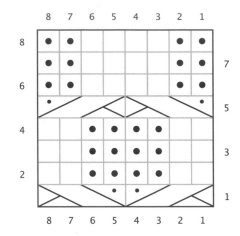

Chart B

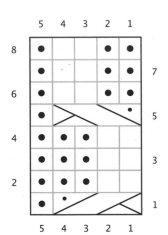

Chart A

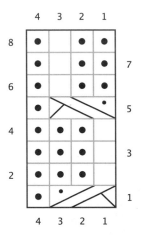

Chart F (Left Sleeve)

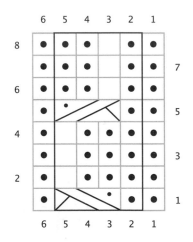

Chart G (Right Sleeve)

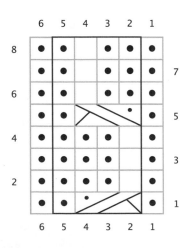

Key

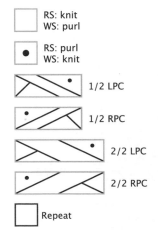

☐	RS: knit WS: purl
•	RS: purl WS: knit
◣	1/2 LPC
◢	1/2 RPC
◣	2/2 LPC
◢	2/2 RPC
☐	Repeat

Hypatia
by Carissa Browning

One Size: 23 cm / 9" deep x 79 cm / 31" circumference
Yarn: Madelinetosh Pashmina (sportweight; 75% merino, 15% silk, 10% cashmere; 329 m / 360 yds per 113 g skein)
Shades:
Yarn A: Copper Pink; 1 skein
Yarn B: Calligraphy; 1 skein
Gauge: 18 sts & 34 rounds = 10 cm / 4" over double-stranded ("marled") garter stitch in the round on 4 mm needles after blocking.
18 sts & 25 rounds = 10 cm / 4" over double-knit stocking stitch in the round on 4 mm needles after blocking.
Note: This will actually be 36 sts, but sts are only counted on one side of the swatch.
Needles: 4 mm / US 6 circular needle, 60 cm / 24" length
Always use a needle size that will result in the correct gauge after blocking.
Notions: Stitch marker, 4 additional stitch markers to mark each repeat of the chart (optional), tapestry needle
Notes: Hypatia uses a mixture of double-stranded ("marled") garter stitch and double knitting in the round. Each double-knit stitch on the chart represents 2 stitches: one knitted using the colour appearing on the chart and the other purled using the other colour. The knit stitches form the front face of the fabric, while the purl stitches form the back face.

Stitch Glossary
[kA, pB]: With both yarns in back, k next st with A, bring both yarns to front, purl next st with B.
[kB, pA]: With both yarns in back, k next st with B, bring both yarns to front, purl next st with A.
mk: K next st with both yarns held together.
mp: P next st with both yarns held together.
mssk: Slip 2 sts knitwise one at a time, knit them together through back loops with both yarns held together.
mssp: Slip 2 sts knitwise one at a time, place them back on LH needle, purl together through back loops with both yarns held together.
splitAB: Split marled st from row below into 2 separate strands for double knitting; with both yarns in back, knit A strand of marled st with A, bring both yarns to front, purl B strand of marled st with B.
splitBA: Split marled st from row below into 2 separate sts for double knitting; with both yarns in back, knit B strand of marled st with B, bring both yarns to front, purl A strand of marled st with A.

CHART - WRITTEN INSTRUCTIONS
For written instructions to use in place of chart, please go to pompommag.com/codes and use the code **bWpvE4Cj** to download.

Hypatia
by Carissa Browning

PATTERN BEGINS

Using the long-tail method and yarns A and B held together, cast on 150 sts.

Join for working in the round being careful not to twist. PM to indicate beg of round.

Note: If desired, PM every 30 sts to indicate beg of each chart repeat.

Commence pattern from Chart or written instructions, working 5 full reps of chart across round, through round 74.

Cast off all sts purlwise, with both yarns held together, removing all markers.

FINISHING

Weave in ends and block to measurements.

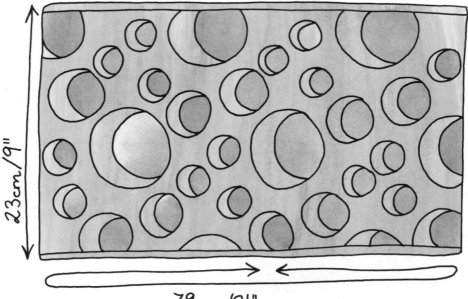

23cm /9"

79cm /31"

Chart

Legend:
- ▨ [kA, pB]
- ☐ [kB, pA]
- ◇ mk
- ◆ mp
- ╲ mssk
- ⟍ mssp
- V split

Sina
by Amy Philip

Sizes: 1 (2, 3)
Finished hand circumference: 19 (20.5, 21.5) cm / 7½ (8, 8½)"
Model wears size 2.
Yarn: Triskelion Yarn Scylfing DK (DK weight; 75% Bluefaced Leicester, 25% Gotland; 230 m / 252 yds per 100 g skein)
Shades:
Yarn A: Thunor's Brow; 1 skein
Yarn B: Prow Dancer; 1 skein
Yarn C: Ember's End; 1 skein
One pair of mitts requires the following approximate quantities:
Yarn A: Thunor's Brow; 15g
Yarn B: Prow Dancer; 35g (40g, 50g)
Yarn C: Ember's End; 35g (40g, 50g)
Gauge: 18 sts & 24 rows = 10 cm / 4" over stocking stitch on 4.5 mm needles with yarns B and C held together after blocking.
Needles: 3.5 mm / US 4 knitting needles suitable for working small circumferences in the round
4.5 mm / US 7 knitting needles suitable for working small circumferences in the round
Always use a needle size that will result in the correct gauge **before** blocking.
Notions: 4 stitch markers, stitch holder or scrap yarn, tapestry needle
Notes: The mittens are knit in the round from the bottom up with the thumb stitches held and picked up at the end. The cuff is worked in rib stitch before changing to stocking stitch for the hand. The hand is worked using one strand of yarn B and one strand of yarn C held double. This allows the moon motif in the centre of the palm to be worked in Fair Isle. When working the moon motif, hold yarn B or yarn C single as indicated in the chart with the unused yarn floating behind it. The pattern for the left and right mitten varies when working the thumb gusset and the moon motif, but the remainder of the pattern is alike for both hands.

Stitch Glossary
1x1 Twisted Rib Stitch (in the round):
Round 1: [K1tbl, p1tbl] to end.
Rep round 1 for pattern.

PATTERN BEGINS
BOTH MITTENS
Note: Both mittens are worked alike to the Thumb Gusset. Using smaller needles, yarn A and the long-tail method, cast on 34 (36, 38) sts. Join for working in the round being careful not to twist. PM to indicate beg of round.

Cuff
Work in 1x1 Twisted Rib Stitch until piece measures 5 cm / 2" from the cast-on edge. Break yarn A.

Hand
Change to larger needles and yarn B and yarn C held together.
Work 5 (7, 9) rounds in St st.

LEFT MITTEN ONLY
Thumb Gusset
Note: During set-up round two sets of markers are placed. The first set mark where to work inc to form the thumb gusset. The second set mark sts where the moon motif is worked. The moon motif is placed on round 10 of the thumb gusset and you will be working from Chart A and working the thumb gusset **AT THE SAME TIME** until the thumb gusset is complete.
Set-up round: K5, PM, k2, PM, k11 (12, 13), PM, k15, PM, k1 (2, 3).
Round 1: K to marker, SM, M1R, k to marker, M1L, SM, [k to marker, SM] twice, k to end. *2 sts inc*
Round 2: Knit.
Rounds 3-9: Rep rounds 1-2 a further 3 times, then round 1 only once more. *44 (46, 48) sts*
Round 10: [K to marker, SM] 3 times, work row 1 of Chart A over next 15 sts, SM, k to end.
Round 11: K5, SM, M1R, k to marker, M1L, SM, k to marker, SM, work next row of Chart A, SM, k to end. *46 (48, 50) sts*
Round 12: [K to marker, SM] 3 times, work next row of Chart A, SM, k to end.

Size 3 ONLY:
Rounds 13-14: Rep rounds 11-12, working next row of Chart A each time. *52 sts*

ALL sizes again
Next round: K5, remove marker, place the next 14 (14, 16) sts onto scrap yarn for thumb, cast on 2 sts using backwards loop method, remove marker, k11 (12, 13), SM, work next row of Chart A, SM, k1 (2, 3). *34 (36, 38) sts*
Next round: K to marker, SM, work next row of Chart A, SM, k to end.
Last round sets patt. Continue in patt as set until Chart A is complete. Continue to "Hand - Both Mittens".

RIGHT MITTEN ONLY
Thumb Gusset
Note: During set-up round two sets of markers are placed. The first set mark sts where the moon motif is worked.

Sina

by Amy Philip

The second set mark where to work inc to form the thumb gusset. The moon motif is placed on round 10 of the thumb gusset and you will be working from Chart B and working the thumb gusset **AT THE SAME TIME** until the thumb gusset is complete.

Set-up round: K1, PM, k15, PM, k11 (12, 13), PM, k2, PM, k5 (6, 7).

Round 1: [K to marker, SM] 3 times, M1R, k to marker, M1L, SM, k to end. *2 sts inc*

Round 2: Knit.

Rounds 3-9: Rep rounds 1-2 a further 3 times, then round 1 only once more. *44 (46, 48) sts*

Round 10: K1, SM, work row 1 of Chart B over next 15 sts, SM, [k to marker, SM] twice, k to end.

Round 11: K1, SM, work next row of Chart B, SM, k to marker, SM, M1R, k to marker, M1L, SM, k to end. *46 (48, 50) sts*

Round 12: K1, SM, work next row of Chart B, SM, [k to marker, SM] twice, k to end.

Size 3 ONLY:

Rounds 13-14: Rep rounds 11-12, working next row of Chart B each time. *52 sts*

ALL sizes again

Next round: K1, SM, work next row of Chart B, SM, k to marker, remove marker, place next 14 (14, 16) sts onto scrap yarn for thumb, cast on 2 sts using backwards loop method, remove marker, k to end. *34 (36, 38) sts*

Next round: K to marker, SM, work next row of Chart B, SM, k to end.

Last round sets patt. Continue in patt as set until Chart B is complete. Continue to "Hand - Both Mittens".

HAND - BOTH MITTENS

Next round: Knit, removing markers.

Continue straight in St st until piece measures 15 (16.5, 17.5) cm / 6 (6½, 7)" from beg of mitten hand, not including cuff.

Shape Mitten Top

Set-up round: K9, PM, k17 (18, 19), PM, k8 (9, 10).

Dec round: *K to 3 sts before marker, ssk, k1, SM, k2tog; rep from * once more, k to end. *4 sts dec*

Rep Dec round a further 5 (6, 6) times, removing markers on last round. *10 (8, 10) sts*

Break yarns B and C, thread yarn tails through rem sts and pull tight to close the mitten top.

THUMB (both mittens alike)

Place 14 (14, 16) held sts onto larger needles, using yarn B and yarn C held together, pick up and k2 sts from 2 backwards loop cast-on sts, k across 14 (14, 16) thumb gusset sts. *16 (16, 18) sts*

Join to work in the round and PM to indicate beg of round.

Work in St st for 5 (5, 5.5) cm / 2 (2, 2¼)".

Dec round: [K2tog] to end. *8 (8, 9) sts*

Break yarns B and C, thread yarn tails through rem sts and pull tight to close the thumb.

FINISHING

Weave in ends and block to measurements.

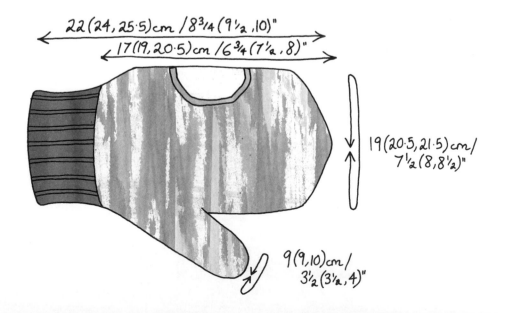

22 (24, 25.5) cm / 8¾ (9½, 10)"

17 (19, 20.5) cm / 6¾ (7½, 8)"

19 (20.5, 21.5) cm / 7½ (8, 8½)"

9 (9, 10) cm / 3½ (3½, 4)"

Chart A (LH Moon)

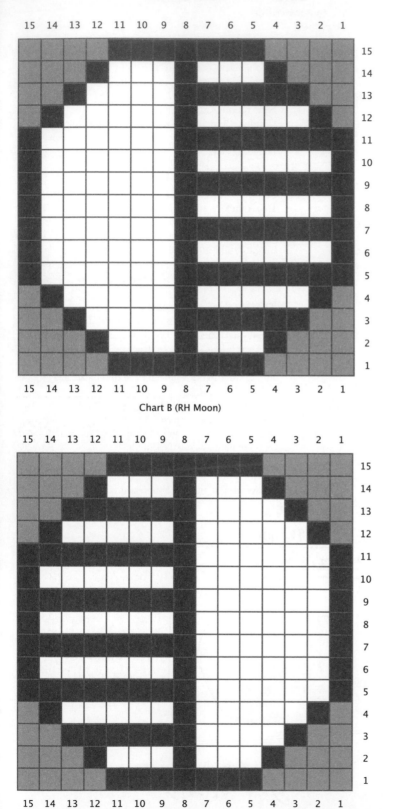

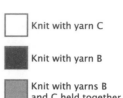

Chart B (RH Moon)

Sina
by Amy Philip

Ixchel
by Catherine Clark

length AND knitting needles suitable for working small circumferences in the round
2.75 mm / US 2 circular needle, 60-80 cm / 24-32" length AND knitting needles suitable for working small circumferences in the round
Always use a needle size that will result in the correct gauge after blocking.
Notions: 11 stitch markers (1 unique for beg of round), stitch holders or scrap yarn, tapestry needle
Notes: Ixchel is a top down yoked colourwork sweater knit in the round. In order to achieve an even fabric, twist the non-working colour at the WS of the work every 2-3 sts. Unlike most yoke sweaters, this one has a centre and back panel that remain untouched by increases. Markers are placed around these panels to remind you and for help with achieving symmetry. Each side of the sweater between front and back panels mirrors the other.
On some rounds of the yoke and when working the main sleeve detail, you will only use yarn B on the centre panels, and yarn A for the rest of the round. To accomplish this, on these rounds break yarn B after completing each panel, leaving a long tail of approximately 65-91 cm / 24-32", depending on number of rows before next fully patterned row. Use a yarn needle to weave the yarn tail back to the beginning of the panel section, ready to be used on the following round. Rejoin yarn B and break yarn B in this way as necessary throughout the pattern.

Stitch Glossary
3x1 Rib (In the round)
Round 1: [K3, p1] to end.
Rep round 1 for pattern.

PATTERN BEGINS
YOKE
Neck
Using smaller needles and yarn A, cast on 108 (108, 120, 128, 128) sts. Join for working in the round being careful not to twist. PM to indicate beg of round.
Work in 3x1 Rib for 9 rounds.
Size 1 ONLY
Next round: *Kfb 3 times, k1, kfb twice, k2; rep from * to last 4 sts, kfb 3 times, k1. *176 sts*
Size 2 ONLY:
Next round: *[Kfb 3 times, k1] 8 times, kfb 4 times; rep from * to end. *192 sts*
Sizes 3 and 4 ONLY
Next round: *Kfb 3 times, k1; rep from * to end. *210 (224) sts*
Size 5 ONLY
Next round: *Kfb 3 times, k1, kfb 4 times; rep from * to end. *240 sts*

Sizes: 1 (2, 3, 4, 5)
Finished bust circumference: 81 (94, 106, 112.5, 125) cm / 32 (37, 41¾, 44¼, 49¼)" – to be worn with 0-10 cm / 0-4" positive ease.
Diana has 94 cm / 37" bust, stands 170 cm / 5'7" tall, is pictured on the front cover, and is wearing a size 3.
Jill has 91 cm / 36" bust, stands 175 cm / 5'9" tall, and is wearing a size 3.
Yarn: Magpie Fibers Swanky Sock (4ply/Fingering weight; Superwash Merino 80%, Cashmere 10%, Nylon 10%; 345 m / 378 yds per 115 g skein)
Shades:
Yarn A: Empty Night; 3 (3, 3, 4, 4) skeins
Yarn B: Moon Beam; 1 (1, 1, 2, 2) skeins
Gauge: 26 sts & 34 rounds = 10 cm / 4" over colourwork pattern on 3.5 mm needles after blocking.
Needles: 3.5 mm / US 4 circular needle, 60-80 cm / 24-32"

Ixchel
by **Catherine Clark**

ALL sizes again
Commence back neck short rows and establish Chart A as foll:

Short row 1 (RS): K12, PM A, k68, k2tog 0 (0, 1, 0, 0) time, w&t.

Short row 2 (WS): P to marker A, SM A, p12, sl beg of round marker, p11, PM D, p68, p2tog 0 (0, 1, 0, 0) time, w&t. *176 (192, 208, 224, 240) sts*

Short row 3 (RS): K to marker D, SM D, work sts 1-11 of row 1 of Chart A to beg of round marker, SM, work sts 12-23 of row 1 of Chart A to marker A, SM A, k59, w&t.

Short row 4 (WS): P to marker A, SM A, reading from left to right work row 2 of Chart A to marker D (slipping beg of round marker as you pass it), SM D, p59, w&t.

Short row 5 (RS): K to marker D, SM D, work next row of Chart A as set to marker A, SM A, k to 10 sts before previous w&t, w&t.

Short row 6 (WS): P to marker A, SM A, work next row of Chart A as set to marker D, SM D, p to 10 sts before previous w&t, w&t.

Rep short rows 5-6 twice more.

Next round (RS): Work in patt to beg of round marker.

BODY

Round 1: Picking up wraps and working them tog with sts as you pass them, reading from right to left work sts 12-23 of row 10 of Chart A, SM A, work row 1 of Chart C 8 (9, 10, 11, 12) times then work first st of Chart C once more, PM B, work row 1 of Chart B once, PM C, work row 1 of Chart C 0 (9, 10, 11, 12) times then work first st of Chart C once more, SM D, work sts 1-11 of row 10 of Chart A.

Note: Round 1 establishes charts between markers, as foll:
Beg of round to Marker A: sts 12-23 of Chart A
Marker A to B: Chart C
Marker B to C: Chart B
Marker C to D: Chart C
Marker D to end of round: sts 1-11 of Chart A
Maintain each chart until otherwise indicated.

Rounds 2-6: Work in patt as set, maintaining charts as est, until Chart A is complete.

Round 7: Work sts 12-23 of row 7 of Chart B, SM A, [patt to marker as set, SM] 3 times, work sts 1-11 of row 7 of Chart B.

Note: You'll now work Chart B from beg of round to Marker A and from Marker D to end of round, as est by last row. All other charts continue as set.

Rounds 8-20: Work in patt as set.

Note: Chart C is now complete.

Size 1 ONLY:
Round 21 (Inc): *Patt to marker, SM, with yarn A [kfb, k3] 16 times, k1, SM; rep from * once more, patt to end. *208 sts*

Size 2 ONLY
Round 21 (Inc): *Patt to marker, SM, with yarn A [kfb, k2, kfb, k3] 10 times, kfb, k2, SM; rep from * once more, patt to end. *234 sts*

Size 3 ONLY
Round 21 (Inc): *Patt to marker, SM, with yarn A kfb, k1, [kfb, k2] 26 times, kfb, SM; rep from * once more, patt to end. *264 sts*

Size 4 ONLY
Round 21 (Inc): *Patt to marker, SM, with yarn A k4, [kfb, k1, kfb, k2] 16 times, k5, SM; rep from * once more, patt to end. *288 sts*

Size 5 ONLY
Round 21 (Inc): *Patt to marker, SM, with yarn A kfb, kfb, [kfb, k2] 31 times, kfb, kfb, SM; rep from * once more, patt to end. *310 sts*

ALL sizes again
Round 22: *Patt to marker, SM, with yarn A k2, work chart D 6 (7, 8, 9, 10) times then work across first 5 (6, 9, 9, 8) sts of chart D once, with yarn A k2, SM; rep from * once more, patt to end.

Round 23: *Patt to marker, SM, with yarn B k1, with yarn A k1, work next row of chart D as set to 2 sts before marker, with yarn A k1, with yarn B k1, SM; rep from * once more, patt to end.

Ixchel
by Catherine Clark

Rounds 24-32: Repeat round 22, working next row of Chart D each time.

Note: Chart D is now complete.

Rounds 33-37: *Patt to marker, SM, work Chart E 20 (23, 27, 30, 33) times, then work first 1 (2, 1, 1, 0) sts of Chart E once, SM; rep from * once more, patt to end.

Note: Chart E is now complete.

Round 38: Patt to marker, SM A, with yarn A k to marker, SM B, patt to marker, SM C, with yarn A k to marker, SM D, patt to end.

Round 39 (Inc): Patt to marker, SM A, with yarn A [kfb, k3] 20 (23, 27, 30, 33) times, kfb, SM B, patt to marker, SM C, with yarn A [kfb, k3] 20 (23, 27, 30, 33) times, kfb 1 (1, 1, 1, 0) times, k0 (1, 0, 0, 0), SM D, patt to end. *250 (282, 320, 350, 376) sts*

Round 40: Patt to marker, SM A, with yarn A k to next marker, SM B, patt to marker, SM C, with yarn A k to next marker, SM D, patt to end.

Round 41: *Patt to marker, SM, work row 1 of chart F across next 30 (39, 39, 39, 39) sts, PM for St st section, with yarn A, k42 (40, 59, 74, 87), PM for St st section, work row 1 of chart G across next 30 (39, 39, 39, 39) sts, SM; rep from * once more, patt to end.

Note: Last round sets new position of charts F and G, with a marked section of St st between them on each side.

Rounds 42-52: Work in patt as set, slipping markers as you pass them.

Note: Charts F and G are now complete.

Round 53: Rep round 38, removing St st section markers.

Round 54 (Inc): *Patt to marker, SM, with yarn A k2 (3, 2, 2, 2), kfb, [k6, kfb] 14 (16, 19, 21, 23) times, k1 (2, 1, 2, 1), SM; rep from * once more, patt to end. *280 (316, 360, 394, 424) sts*

Note: As you work the next round, for **sizes 2 and 4** ONLY evenly decrease - (2, -, 1, -) sts in **each** Chart H section (between markers A and B, and C and D). - *(312, -, 392, -) sts*

Rounds 55-60: *Patt to marker, SM, work Chart H to 1 st before next marker, then work first st of Chart H once, SM; rep from * once more, patt to end.

Note: Chart H is now complete.

Separate sleeves and body:

Round 61: Patt to marker, SM A, with yarn A k33 (39, 47, 52, 58), place next 51 (55, 63, 69, 73) sts on holder for Sleeve, cast on 15 (15, 15, 17, 17) sts for underarm, k33 (39, 47, 52, 58), SM B, patt to marker, SM C, with yarn A k33 (39, 47, 52, 58) sts, place next 51 (55, 63, 69, 73) sts on holder for Sleeve, cast on 15 (15, 15, 17, 17) sts for underarm, k33 (39, 47, 52, 58), SM D, patt to end. *208 (232, 264, 288, 312) sts; 23 sts for Front and Back centre panels, 81 (93, 109, 121, 133) sts between markers A and B, and markers C and D.*

Note: As you work the next round, for sizes **2, 3 and 5** ONLY, evenly inc 4 sts in **each** Chart I section (between markers A and B, and C and D). *208 (240, 272, 288, 320) sts; 23 sts for Front and Back centre panels, 81 (97, 113, 121, 137) sts between markers A and B, and markers C and D.*

Rounds 62-69: *Patt to marker, SM, with yarn A k0 (2, 4, 2, 4), work chart I 6 (7, 8, 9, 10) times then work first 9 sts of chart I once, with yarn A k0 (2, 4, 2, 4), SM; rep from * once more, patt to end.

Round 70: *Patt to marker, SM, with yarn B k0 (1, 1, 1, 1), with yarn A k0 (1, 3, 1, 3), work chart I as set to last 0 (2, 4, 2, 4) sts before marker, with yarn A k0 (1, 3, 1, 3), with yarn B k0 (1, 1, 1, 1), SM; rep from * once more, patt to end.

Rounds 71-72: Rep round 62, working next row of Chart I each time.

Note: Chart I is now complete.

Rounds 73-84: *Patt to marker, SM, work chart J once, work chart L 7 (9, 11, 12, 14) times then work first st of chart L once more, work chart K once; rep from * once more, patt to end.

Rounds 85-104: *Patt to marker, SM, work Chart L to 1 st before marker then work first st of chart L once more, SM; rep from * once more, patt to end.

Note: Chart B is now complete.

Round 105-120: Work next row of Chart L to end, removing all markers on first round except beg of round marker.

Rounds 121-160: Work Chart M to end.

Round 161: With yarn A, knit.

Note: Additional rows can be worked in yarn A here to add length if desired.

Change to smaller needles.

Work in 3x1 rib for 21 rounds or to desired length.

Change to larger needles. Cast off in rib.

SLEEVES

Using yarn A and larger needles suitable for working small circumferences in the round, beg at the center of underarm, pick up and knit 1 st, PM, pick up and knit 7 (7, 7, 8, 8) sts, knit across held 51 (55, 63, 69, 73) Sleeve sts working final held st as kfb (kfb, k1, kfb, kfb), pick up and knit 7 (7, 7, 8, 8) sts, PM to indicate beg of round. *67 (71, 78, 87, 91) sts*

Round 1: With yarn A, knit and **at the same** time evenly inc 3 (3, 0, 1, 7) sts across the round. *70 (74, 78, 88, 98) sts*

Rounds 2-12: With yarn A k1, SM, k1, work sts 3-12 of chart I once, then work sts 1-12 of chart I to end.

Note: Pattern will not be continuous at underarm, and you will not end with a complete repeat of chart.

Right Sleeve ONLY

Rounds 13-16: Work from Chart L to end, beg on row 7 and st 3, working rows 7-10 only.

Ixchel
by **Catherine Clark**

Left Sleeve ONLY
Rounds 13-16: Work from Chart L to end, beg on row 7 and st 7, working rows 7-10 only.

BOTH sleeves
Rounds 17-18: With yarn A, knit.
Round 19: Work row 12 of Chart L to end, beg at correct starting point for Right or Left Sleeve as before.
Round 20: With yarn A, k1, SM, k30 (32, 34, 39, 44), PM A, k9, PM B, k to end.
Round 21: With yarn A, knit, slipping markers as you pass them.
Please read the following section carefully as you will be working two sets of instructions **AT THE SAME TIME**.
Rounds 22-131: With yarn A, k1, SM, knit to marker, SM, join yarn B and work chart N to marker, break yarn B leaving a 91 cm / 36" tail, SM, with yarn A k to end.
Note: Do not carry yarn B around sleeve. Instead, weave yarn B tail back with a yarn needle to beg of chart on each row. When yarn B runs out, attach another segment of same length. Continue adding more segments of yarn B as needed throughout.

AT THE SAME TIME work Sleeve shaping, beginning on round 21 as foll:

Dec round: K1, SM, k2tog tbl, patt to last 2 sts, k2tog.
2 sts dec
Rep Dec round every 7th (7th, 8th, 7th, 6th) round a further 12 (12, 12, 13, 16) times. *44 (48, 52, 60, 64) sts*
Continue straight in pattern, working in St st with yarn A once Chart N is complete, until sleeve measures 36 cm / 14" or 7.5 cm / 3" less than desired length.
Change to smaller needles suitable for working small circumferences in the round.
Work in 3x1 Rib for 7.5 cm / 3".
Change to larger needles.
Cast off in rib.

Finishing:
Weave in all ends paying careful attention to closing any holes in each underarm. Block to measurements.

a. Bust circumference: 81 (94, 106, 112.5, 125) cm / 32 (37, 41¾, 44¼, 49¼)"
b. Neck width: 15, 15, 16.5, 17.5, 17.5 cm / 6 (6, 6½, 7, 7)"
c. Upper arm circumference: 27 (29, 30.5, 34, 38) cm / 10¾ (11½, 12, 13½, 15)"
d. Sleeve length: 43.5 cm / 17"
e. Length (underarm to hem): 36 cm / 14¼"

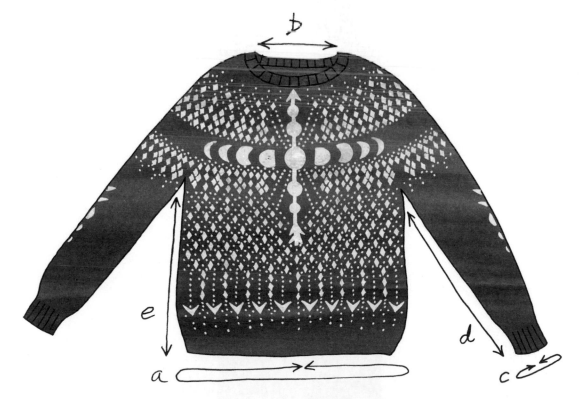

Ixchel
by Catherine Clark

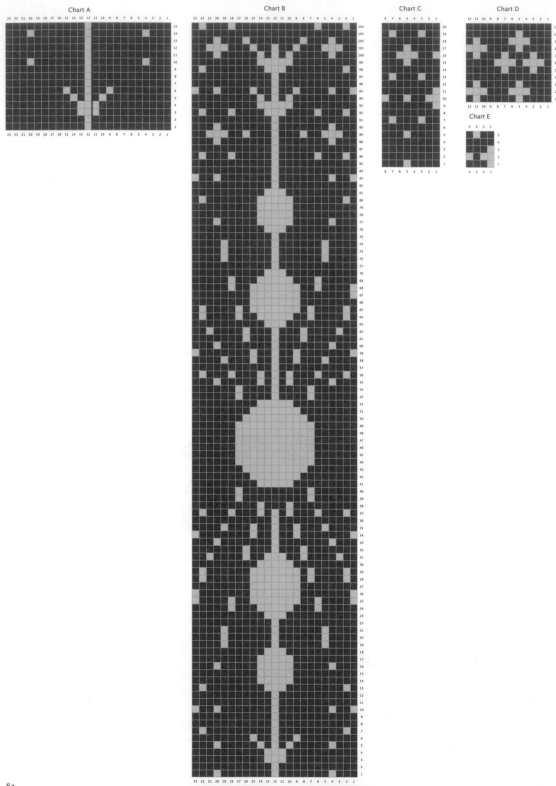

Chart A

Chart B

Chart C

Chart D

Chart E

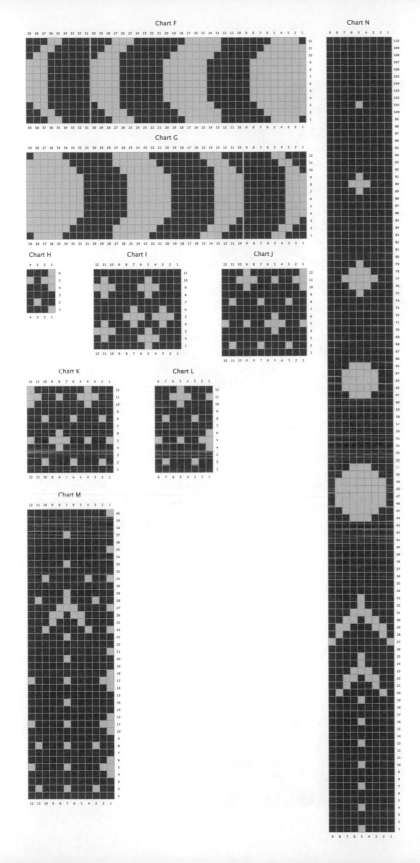

To download and print a large scale version of these charts, please go to pompommag.com/codes and use the code **JqRqeq8k**.

Sky Map

by **Emily Foden**

One size: 213 cm / 84" long x 48.5 cm / 19" wide
Yarn: Viola Mohair Lace (lace weight; 72% mohair, 28% silk; 420 m / 459 yds per 50 g skein)
Shades:
Yarn A: Cosmic; 4 skeins
Yarn B: Garden Ghost; 1 skein
Note: Approximately 10 g is required for yarn B.
Gauge: 23 sts & 29 rounds = 10 cm / 4" over stocking stitch in the round on 4 mm needles after blocking.
Needles: 4 mm / US 6 circular needle, 80 cm / 32" length. Always use a needle size that will result in the correct gauge after blocking.
Notions: 2 stitch markers, split ring markers, small tapestry needle for embroidery.
Notes: The Sky Map Shawl is knit in the round from end to end in stocking stitch creating a rectangular shawl made up of two layers of knitting. Faux seams run along the sides of the shawl. After knitting and blocking both layers flat, yarn B is used to stitch stars, constellations and moons through both layers of knitting, creating a quilted effect. Tassels are then attached along the short edges of the shawl.

The layout and placement of stars is entirely up to the knitter. Please do not feel limited to the sample design, but also feel free to use any aspect of the design that suits you. This is a chance to stitch exactly what and where you please. It's basically a chance to draw on your knitting! Experienced embroiderers may want to incorporate other types of stitches and techniques, while a novice should feel free to dive in with confidence.

Stitch Glossary

Running Stitch: Stitch through both layers of knitting using short (approx. 0.5 cm / ¼") in stitches. Take care that running stitches are tidy on both sides of work, as they will be visible from both front and back.
Criss Cross Stars: Formed by overlapping several individual stitches in different directions.
Burst Stars: Formed by individual stitches radiating out from a central point.
Moons, shapes and lines: Use travelling running stitches to create any desired shape. Build up lines of stitches or fill in shapes if desired.
Make Tassel: See pompommag.com/tutorials for a visual guide to making tassels.

PATTERN BEGINS
SHAWL

Using long tail method and yarn A, cast on 244 sts. Join for working for the round, being careful not to twist sts. PM to indicate beg of round.
Set-up Round: K121, p1, PM, K to last st, p1.

Round 1: [K to 1 st before marker, p1, SM] twice.
Rep round 1 until piece measures approximately 213 cm / 84" from cast-on edge. Cast off all sts loosely. Weave in ends and block to measurements.

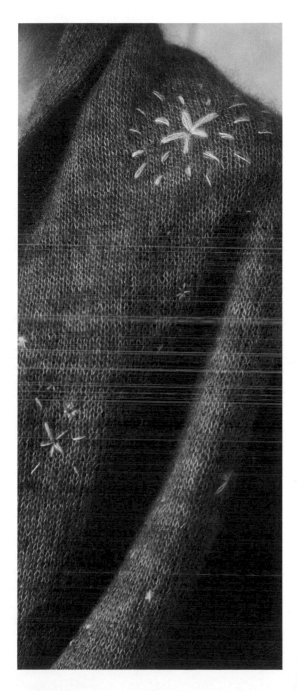

Sky Map
by Emily Foden

Stitching

Using split ring markers, or safety pins, pin together top and bottom layers of work before stitching - space out pins evenly, ensuring that entire piece lays flat and is anchored together before stitching into it.

Using small tapestry needle threaded with a length of yarn B, either single or double stranded, stitch your desired pattern. Sample uses a single strand of yarn B for small stars and two strands together for larger stars. Leaving a short tail of yarn B on RS of work for every length of yarn B used, stitch as many, or as few stars as you would like. When length of yarn is used up, thread tail onto needle, loop through nearest star, thread tail through loop forming a knot. Tuck to inside of work. Do the same at the end of every length of yarn.

Keep stitches tidy on front and back of work, as both sides will be visible when piece is worn. Alternating between front and back facing while stitching will help to ensure tidiness on both sides. You may sneak yarn B from one star to the next on the inside of work. The trail of yarn between layers of knitting will be barely visible.

Secure ends of yarn B with knot, and tuck tails to inside of work.

FINISHING

Make 10 tassels. Attach 5 tassels to each end, evenly spaced across cast-on and cast-off edges.

213cm/84"

48.5cm /19"

Sky Map
by Emily Foden

EMBROIDERY NOTES

RUNNING STITCH

wears in when stitching is finished

Stitch through both layers of Knitting using short (approx 0.5cm /¼") stitches. Take care that running stitches are tidy on both sides of work as they'll be visible from front & back.

CRISS-CROSS STARS

Formed by overlapping several individual stitches in different directions.

BURST STARS

Formed by individual stitches radiating out from a central point.

MOONS, SHAPES & LINES

Use travelling running stitches to create any desired shape. Build up lines of stitches or fill in shapes... have fun!

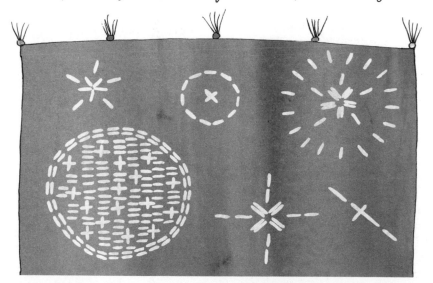

Moonbow
by Jule Kebelmann

Sizes: 1 (2, 3, 4, 5, 6)

Finished bust circumference: 92 (100, 108, 116, 124, 132) cm / 36¼ (39½, 42½, 45½, 48¾, 52)" – to be worn with 12-23 cm / 4¾-9" positive ease

Diana has 94 cm / 37" bust, stands 170 cm / 5'7" tall, is pictured on page X and is wearing a size 4.

Jenny has 91 cm / 36" bust, stands 173 cm / 5'8" tall, is pictured on page X and is wearing a size 4.

Yarn A: Hey Mama Wolf Schafwolle No.03 (sport weight; 100% wool; 260 m / 284 yds per 100 g skein)
Shade: Dark Indigo; 5 (6, 6, 6, 7, 7) skeins

Yarn B: Hey Mama Wolf Sockyarn No.04 (sock weight; 80% wool; 20% ramie; 300 m / 382 yds per 100 g skein)
Shade: Amethyst; 1 mini skein set of five colours: 1, 2, 3, 4, 5

Gauge: 23 sts & 32 rows = 10 cm / 4" over Stocking stitch on 2.5 mm needles after blocking.

Needles: 2.5 mm / US 2 circular needle, 80 cm / 32" length
Always use a needle size that will result in the correct gauge after blocking.

Notions: 1 stitch marker, scrap yarn or stitch holders, tapestry needle

Notes: Moonbow is knitted in pieces and sewn after knitting and blocking. The front and back pieces are knitted from the bottom up including the hem. Sleeves are worked sideways from the sleeve cuff towards the centre back/front leaving an opening for the head. The two sets of live stitches are then joined using Kitchener stitch before sewing the sleeve and side seams and the seams that join sleeves and body. The fringe on the front piece is added as you go. The neckband is picked up and knitted after all pieces are joined.

Insert fringes
Cut the yarn into approx. 18 – 20 cm / 7 – 8" long pieces. Before working the next st lay a piece of yarn over the needle and pull the end that lays on the WS to the RS between the needles. Work the st, catching the fringe between the sts. After knitting the whole row, trim the fringes to 7 cm / 2¾".

PATTERN BEGINS
BACK
Using the long-tail method and yarn A, cast on 108 (116, 124, 136, 144, 152) sts.
Row 1 (WS): [K1, p1] to end.
Rows 2-9: Rep row 1.
Next row (RS): Knit.
Short row 1 (WS): P to last 4 sts, w&t.
Short row 2 (RS): K to last 4 sts, w&t.
Short row 3: P to 4 sts before w&t, w&t.
Short row 4: K to 4 sts before w&t, w&t.
Next row: P to end, working wraps tog with sts as you pass them.
Next row: K to end, working wraps tog with sts as you pass them.
Continue in St st for a further 80 (80, 80, 78, 78, 78) rows. Shape top of back as foll:
Cast off 6 (6, 7, 8, 8, 8) sts at beg of next 2 rows. *96 (104, 110, 120, 128, 136) sts*
Cast off 2 sts on the beg of the next 14 (10, 6, 6, 4, 6) rows. *68 (84, 98, 108, 120, 124) sts*
Cast off 3 sts on the beg of the next 4 (6, 8, 8, 12, 4) rows. *56 (66, 74, 84, 84, 112) sts*
Cast off 4 sts on the beg of the next 6 (8, 10, 12, 12, 18) rows.
Cast off remaining 32 (34, 34, 36, 36, 40) sts.

FRONT
Using the long-tail method and yarn A, cast on 108 (116, 124, 136, 144, 152) sts.
Row 1 (WS): [K1, p1] to end.
Rows 2-9: Rep row 1.
Continue in St st for a further 84 (84, 84, 82, 82, 82) rows.

Moonbow
by Jule Kebelmann

Shape top of Front and add fringe as foll:

Row 1 (RS): Using first shade of yarn B for fringe and yarn A as working yarn, cast off 6 (6, 7, 8, 8, 8) sts (1 st on RH needle after cast off), k1, knit 11 (13, 13, 13, 16, 16) sts with fringes (see Pattern Notes), k to last 19 (21, 22, 23, 26, 26) sts, knit 11 (13, 13, 13, 16, 16) sts with fringes, k to end. *102 (110, 117, 128, 136, 144) sts*

Row 2 (WS): Cast off 6 (6, 7, 8, 8, 8) sts, p to end. *96 (104, 110, 120, 128, 136) sts*

Rows 3-4: Cast off 2 sts, patt to end. *92 (100, 106, 116, 124, 132) sts*

Row 5: Using second shade of yarn B for fringe and yarn A as working yarn, cast off 2 sts (1 st on RH needle after cast off), k1, knit 11 (16, 14, 14, 18, 17) sts with fringes, k to last 15 (20, 18, 18, 22, 21) sts, knit 11 (16, 14, 14, 18, 17) sts with fringes, k to end. *90 (98, 104, 114, 122, 130) sts*

Row 6: Cast off 2 sts, patt to end. *88 (96, 102, 112, 120, 128) sts*

Rows 7-8: Cast off 2 (2, 2, 2, 3, 2) sts, patt to end. *84 (92, 98, 108, 114, 124) sts*

Row 9: Using third shade of yarn B for fringe and yarn A as working yarn, cast off 2 (2, 3, 2, 3, 3) sts (1 st on RH needle after cast off), k1, knit 13 (17, 16, 15, 20, 20) sts with fringes, knit to last 17 (21, 21, 19, 25, 25) sts, knit 13 (17, 16, 15, 20, 20) sts with fringes, k to end. *82 (90, 95, 106, 111, 121) sts*

Rows 10-12: Cast off 2 (2, 3, 2, 3, 3) sts, patt to end. *76 (84, 86, 100, 102, 112) sts*

Row 13: Using 4th (4th, 4th, 3rd, 3rd, 3rd) shade of yarn B for fringe and yarn A as working yarn, cast off 2 (3, 3, 2, 3, 4) sts (1 st on RH needle after cast off), k1, knit 15 (17, 15, 15, 21, 19) sts with fringes, k to last 19 (22, 20, 19, 26, 25) sts, knit 15 (17, 15, 15, 21, 19) sts with fringes, k to end. *74 (81, 83, 98, 99, 108) sts*

Row 14: Cast off 2 (3, 3, 2, 3, 4) sts, patt to end. *72 (78, 80, 96, 96, 104) sts*

Rows 15-16: Cast off 2 (3, 3, 3, 3, 4) sts, patt to end. *68 (72, 74, 90, 90, 96) sts*

Row 17: Using fourth shade of yarn B for fringe and yarn A as working yarn, cast off 3 (3, 4, 3, 3, 4) sts (1 st on RH needle after cast off), k1, knit 15 (16, 16, 19, 20, 20) sts with fringes, k to last 20 (21, 22, 24, 25, 26) sts, knit 15 (16, 16, 19, 20, 20) sts with fringes, k to end. *65 (69, 70, 87, 87, 92) sts*

Row 18: Cast off 3 (3, 4, 3, 3, 4) sts, patt to end. *62 (66, 66, 84, 84, 88) sts*

Rows 19-20: Cast off 3 (4, 4, 4, 4, 4) sts, patt to end. *56 (58, 58, 76, 76, 80) sts*

Row 21: Using 5th (5th, 5th, 4th, 4th, 4th) shade of yarn B for fringe and yarn A as working yarn, cast off 4 sts (1 st on RH needle after cast off), k1, knit 13 (13, 13, 17, 17, 19) sts with fringes, k to last 19 (19, 19, 23, 23, 25) sts, knit 13 (13, 13, 17, 17, 19) sts with fringes, k to end. *52 (54, 54, 72, 72, 76) sts*

Rows 22-23: Cast off 4 sts, patt to end. *44 (46, 46, 64, 64, 68) sts*

Sizes 1, 2 & 3 ONLY

Row 24 (WS): Using fifth shade of yarn B for fringe and yarn A as working yarn, cast off 4 sts (1 st on RH needle after cast off), p9 (10, 10, -, -, -), purl 20 sts with fringes, p to end. *40 (42, 42, -, -, -) sts*

Row 25: Cast off 4 sts, patt to end. *36 (38, 38, -, -, -) sts*

Row 26 (WS): Using fifth shade of yarn B for fringe and yarn A as working yarn, cast off 4 sts (1 st on RH needle after cast off), p1, purl 28 (30, 30, -, -, -) sts with fringes, p to end. *32 (34, 34, -, -, -) sts*

Sizes 4, 5 & 6 ONLY

Row 24 (WS): Cast off 4 sts, patt to end. *- (-, -, 60, 60, 64) sts*

Row 25 (RS): Using fifth shade of yarn B for fringe and yarn A as working yarn, cast off 4 sts (1 st on RH needle after cast off), k1, knit - (-, -, 14, 14, 16) sts with fringes, k to last - (-, -, 20, 20, 22) sts, knit - (-, -, 14, 14, 16) sts with fringes, k to end. *- (-, 56, 56, 60) sts*

Rows 26-27: Cast off 4 sts, patt to end. *- (-, -, 48, 48, 52) sts*

Row 28 (WS): Using fifth shade of yarn B for fringe and yarn A as working yarn, cast off 4 sts (1 st on RH needle after cast off), p- (-, -, 11, 11, 13), purl 20 sts with fringes, p to end. *- (-, -, 44, 44, 48) sts*

Row 29 (RS): Cast off 4 sts, patt to end. *- (-, -, 40, 40, 44) sts*

Row 30 (WS): Using fifth shade of yarn B for fringe and yarn A as working yarn, cast off 4 sts (1 st on RH needle after cast off), p1, purl - (-, -, 32, 32, 36) sts with fringes, p to end. *- (-, -, 36, 36, 40) sts*

ALL Sizes again

Cast off rem 32 (34, 34, 36, 36, 40) sts.

LEFT SLEEVE

Using the long-tail method and yarn A, cast on 22 (24, 25, 25, 26, 27) sts, PM, cast on 22 (24, 25, 25, 26, 27) sts. *44 (48, 50, 50, 52, 54) sts*

Row 1 (WS): [K1, p1] to end.

Rows 2-9: Rep row 1.

Note: Read the following instructions carefully as you will be working multiple sets of instructions **at the same time.**

Inc row (RS): K to 1 st before marker, M1R, k1, SM, k1, M1L, k to end. *2 sts inc*

Rep Inc Row every 6th row a further 10 (10, 5, 15, 14, 15) times, then every 8th row 15 (15, 20, 12, 13, 12) times. *52 (52, 52, 56, 56, 56) sts inc in total*

Moonbow
by Jule Kebelmann

AT THE SAME TIME
When sleeve measures 53 (52, 52, 51, 51, 49) cm / 21 (20¼, 20½, 20, 20, 19½)" from cast-on edge ending with a WS row, shape underarm:
Cast off 6 (6, 7, 8, 8, 8) sts at beg of next 2 rows.
Dec row (RS): K2, k2tog, k to last 4 sts, ssk, k2. *2 sts dec*
Rep Dec Row every 4th row a further 4 (6, 1, 5, 0, 0) times, then every 8th row 0 (0, 0, 0, 3, 1) times, then every 6th row 5 (5, 9, 7, 5, 10) times. *20 (24, 22, 26, 18, 24) sts dec in total*

AT THE SAME TIME
When sleeve measures 65 (65, 67, 68, 63, 63) cm / 25¾ (25¾, 26½, 27, 25, 25)" from cast-on edge ending with a WS row, shape Upper Left Front and Upper Left Back sections:
Next row (RS): Patt to marker (including edge Dec as necessary), remove marker, cast off next 16 (16, 16, 16, 17, 17) sts, patt to end. Continue on these sts only for Upper Left Front section, placing rem sts on hold for Upper Left Back.

Upper Left Front section:
Next row (WS): Purl.
Cast off 1 st at beg of every RS row 5 (3, 5, 5, 7, 5) times.
Cast off 1 st at beg of every foll 4th row 0 (2, 1, 1, 0, 1) times.
Continue in St st for a further 22 (22, 23, 22, 25, 25) rows.
Break yarn. Place rem 11 (11, 11, 10, 13, 12) sts on stitch holder or scrap yarn.

Upper Left Back section:
With WS facing, rejoin yarn to Upper Left Back sts.
Continue in St st until Upper Left Back section length measures same as Upper Left Front section.
Break yarn. Place rem 32 (32, 33, 32, 37, 35) sts on a stitch holder or scrap yarn.

RIGHT SLEEVE
Using the long-tail method and yarn A, cast on 22 (24, 25, 25, 26, 27) sts, PM, cast on 22 (24, 25, 25, 26, 27) sts. *44 (48, 50, 50, 52, 54) sts*
Row 1 (WS): [K1, p1] to end.
Rows 2-9: Rep Row 1.
Note: Read the following instructions carefully as you will be working multiple sets of instructions **at the same time.**
Inc row (RS): K to 1 st before marker, M1R, K1, SM, K1, M1L, k to end. *2 sts inc*
Rep Inc Row every 6th row a further 10 (10, 5, 15, 14, 15) times, then every 8th row 15 (15, 20, 12, 13, 12) times. *52 (52, 52, 56, 56, 56) sts inc in total*

AT THE SAME TIME
When sleeve measures 53 (51.5, 52, 51, 51, 49) cm / 21 (20¼, 20½, 20, 20, 19½)" from cast-on edge ending with a WS row, shape underarm:
Cast off 6 (6, 7, 8, 8, 8) sts at beg of next 2 rows.
Dec row (RS): K2, k2tog, k to last 4 sts, ssk, k2. *2 sts dec*
Rep Dec Row every 4th row a further 4 (6, 1, 5, 0, 0) times, then every 8th row 0 (0, 0, 0, 3, 1) times, then every 6th row 5 (5, 9, 7, 5, 10) times. *20 (24, 22, 26, 18, 24) sts dec in total*

AT THE SAME TIME
When sleeve measures 65 (65, 67, 68, 63, 63) cm / 25¾ (25¾, 26½, 27, 25, 25)" from cast-on edge ending with a RS row, shape Upper Right Front and Upper Right Back sections:
Next row (WS): Patt to marker, remove marker, cast off next 16 (16, 16, 16, 17, 17) sts, patt to end. Continue on these sts only for Upper Right Front section, placing rem sts on hold for Upper Right Back.

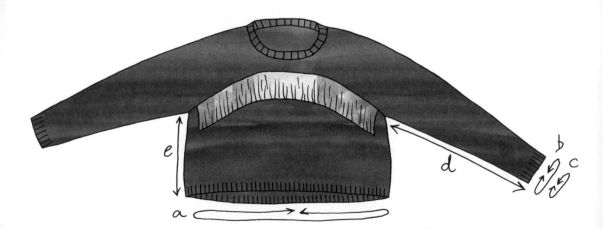

Moonbow
by **Jule Kebelmann**

Upper Right Front section:
Next row (RS): Knit.
Cast off 1 st at beg of every WS row 5 (3, 5, 5, 7, 5) times.
Cast off 1 st at beg of every foll 4th row 0 (2, 1, 1, 0, 1) times.
Continue in St st for a further 23 (23, 24, 23, 26, 26) rows.
Break yarn. Place rem 11 (11, 11, 10, 13, 12) sts on a stitch holder or scrap yarn.

Upper Right Back section:
With RS facing, rejoin yarn to Upper Right Back sts.
Continue in St st until Upper Right Back section length measures same as Upper Right Front section.
Break yarn. Place rem 32 (32, 33, 32, 37, 35) sts on a stitch holder or scrap yarn.

FINISHING
Weave in ends and block to measurements. Join the Upper Front and Upper Back sections of sleeves using Kitchener stitch. Seam sleeves and sides of the body pieces using mattress stitch. With contrasting scrap yarn, baste sleeves to body, then seam using back stitch.

Neckband
With RS facing, beg at left shoulder, pick up and k39 (37, 39, 40, 42, 42) sts to centre Front neck, pick up and k39 (37, 39, 40, 42, 42) sts up to right shoulder, pick up and k70 (74, 74, 74, 76, 80) sts along Back neck. Join to work in the round, being careful not to twist. PM to indicate beg of round. *148 (148, 152, 154, 160, 164) sts*
Rib round: [K1, p1] to end.
Rep Rib round a further 7 times. Cast off.
Weave in ends.

a. Bust circumference: 92 (100, 108, 116, 124, 132) cm / 36¼ (39½, 42½, 45½, 48¾, 52)"
b. Upper arm circumference: 39.5 (40.5, 40.5, 42, 42.5, 43) cm / 15½ (16, 16, 16¼, 16½, 16¾)"
c. Wrist circumference: 18.5 (19.5, 20, 20.5, 21, 21.5) cm / 7¼ (7½, 7¾, 8, 8¼, 8½)"
d. Sleeve length: 59 (59, 60, 60.5, 61, 61) cm / 23¼ (23¼, 23½, 23¾, 24, 24)"
e. Length (hem to underarm): 29 (29, 29, 28.5, 28.5, 28.5) cm / 11½ (11½, 11½, 11¼, 11¼, 11¼)"

MAKING MOON GARLANDS

The Viola team made our first moon garlands for Pomfest in summer 2017 as a decoration for the Viola stand. Not only were they fun to make, but they're also compact and lightweight, making them easy to transport from Canada to the UK and back again. Since Pomfest, we've made many more moon garlands. They have decorated Viola's office, windows, and even Christmas tree!

If you're anything like me, the thrill of gazing at the moon never goes away. Just like the real thing, these moon garlands are always moving and changing. They subtly spin, flicker, and cast drifting celestial shadows on their surroundings, providing a little bit of moon magic wherever they hang.

words and images by **Emily Foden of Viola Yarns**

Shape templates for you to trace around.

Materials

- Watercolour or mixed media paper, approx. 250 gsm or above. Choose something that will be heavy enough to hold its shape when cut out, and not pucker or curl when wet. We used 30.5 cm x 45.7 cm (12 x 18") sheets. One sheet will make about 6 metres of garland, depending on distribution and size of pieces.

- Paints. Any combination of gouache, watercolour, acrylic works nicely. For added shimmer, use a metallic medium such as Golden's Interference Gold paint.

- Paint brushes in a variety of sizes and shapes, and sponges for applying paint.

- Stencils for tracing moon shapes onto your painted paper. Make these from cardboard or heavy card stock using the template provided on page 93.

- Scissors.

- Pom poms. Refer to pompommag.com/pom-pom-garland and make approx 3-5 pom poms for every 2.5 metres of garland, ranging from 5 cm (2") to 9 cm (3.5") in diameter.

- Sewing needle. Aim for the smallest needle possible with your choice of thread.

- Thread. Example uses Valdani 3-ply cotton Embroidery Floss, but fine crochet cotton is also a good choice.

- Pencil. Preferably a hard pencil such as 2H that will create faint lines on your painted paper.

- Thimble (optional) for delicate fingers or anyone who wants to make lots and lots of garlands.

Fig.1

Fig.2

Fig.3

Fig.4

Fig.5

Fig.6

Method

1. Paint your paper! There are no rules here, just grab your paints and start experimenting with colour, placement, and shape. You can't do this step wrong! Even if you're not happy with the way a page has come out, it will take on a new life when you cut it up, so be daring. I like to start with a wash of water, and gradually apply layers of paint that bleed together and combine to make amazing colours. Paint as many sheets as you need to achieve the length of garland you want. (*Fig. 1*)

Let your painted sheets dry, and repeat on the reverse. All sheets must be painted on BOTH sides. Let sheets dry before moving onto the next step. (*Fig. 2*)

2. Trace around stencils onto your painted paper using a faint pencil line. You will be able to fit quite a lot of moons on each page, and it's up to you to choose how many pieces of each shape and size you want. I prefer to make lots of small moons, and use just a few large pieces as an accent. (*Fig. 3*)

3. Cut out moons! Hang onto the misshapen little 'in between' pieces; they look like little stars and fill in gaps nicely when stringing the garland. (*Fig. 4+5*)

4. Make some pom poms! You won't need many; just a few go a long way. Refer to pompommag.com/pom-pom-garland for directions. Ensure that two long strands remain on each pom pom, you will use these to tie them onto the garland. (*Fig. 6*)

5. Thread your needle and start stringing moons!

Space out pieces on average 13 cm / 5" to 23 cm / 9" apart, or to your preference. I preferred to leave a good amount of space between each piece, leaving just the odd pair close together. To mix up the orientation of your moons, insert your needle into varying points in the pieces (e.g. centre, top, bottom, sides). (*Fig. 7+8*) To ensure that moons hang facing all directions, thread some pieces straight through once and pull thread through twice on others. (*Fig. 9*)

If you plan to make a very long garland, it is best to make several shorter lengths. Tie these separate lengths together when you are ready to put them up, thus avoiding a very tangled moon mess.

6. Tie on pom poms. Space them out as you would like across the garland, adjusting the placement of paper pieces as needed. Bear in mind that the pom poms are quite a bit heavier than the paper moons and will weigh down the garland wherever you place them. If possible, I like to tie on pom poms when the garland is in place. This way, you can find the perfect place for them. Their added weight can be helpful when displaying as it secures ends and adds drape. (*Fig. 10*)

7. Hang up your garland and enjoy! (*Fig. 11*)

p.s. When they're not in use, I gently wrap the garlands around a piece of cardboard and tuck them away for safe and tangle-free storage.

Fig.7

Fig.8

Fig.9

Fig.10

Fig.11

MOONSET PANCAKE

The sun rises as the moon sets and breakfast is on most of our minds. But most of us aren't awake enough for a fuss in the kitchen. Rebecca suggests her version of a Dutch Baby pancake for lazy Sunday mornings when you want something indulgent but stress-free. It even looks like the moon!

Night owls will love this recipe as much as early birds because the process is simpler and the results more comforting than garter stitch. You can even make the batter as the moon rises the night before and store it in the fridge until morning. The easy batter makes an impressive brunch dish for sharing with gods and goddesses like your best knitting friends.

- 1 large egg
- 1 tsp caster sugar
- 50 ml / 6 tbsp full fat milk
- 35 g / 4 tbsp plain flour
- generous pinch freshly grated nutmeg
- generous pinch cinnamon or mixed spice
- 12 g / 1 tbsp unsalted butter
- small handful of hazelnuts (roughly 12 nuts)
- one peach or pear, peeled, cored and sliced into eighths
- 2 tsp salted butter
- 2 tsp maple syrup
- optional toppings: berries, mascarpone, icing (powdered) sugar

You will need an ovenproof individual frying pan or skillet (like an omelette pan).

Preheat the oven to 220°C / 425°F, and place your pan into the oven to heat up while you prep the batter.

Beat the egg with the sugar until light and frothy. Whisk in the milk, flour, and spices and continue whisking until you have a smooth thin batter.

Remove the pan from the oven, carefully put the butter into the hot pan and swirl to melt, then quickly pour in the batter and return it to the oven. It will seem like a lot of butter, but it's worth it!

Bake until puffed and golden brown, about 10–12 minutes.

While the batter is baking, prepare the hazelnuts and peaches or pears. Take a dry frying pan and place on a gentle heat. Add the hazelnuts and move them around the pan until lightly toasted. Just as they are starting to turn golden, remove them from the pan and onto a chopping board, leave to cool slightly then roughly chop them.

Keeping the pan on the stove, add the salted butter and, once melted, add the maple syrup, stir together and then add the slices of peach or pear. Toss around the pan until they are coated and cook gently until they're just softening and sitting in a lovely caramel sauce – around 5 minutes. Turn down the heat and leave until the Dutch Baby is ready.

Remove the Dutch Baby from the oven when puffed and golden, gently turn out onto a plate and top with the pears, hazelnuts, and any additional toppings.

recipe by **Rebecca Lawrence**
image by **Juju Vail**

THE
GODDESSES

Our Issue 26 Contributers

image by Emily Foden

Amy Philip is a Brighton-based mum of three, knitwear designer, and lover of all things handmade. She is the designer, and maker behind Button and Blue, her award-winning brand of knitwear for little ones, known for its contemporary and playful designs, knitting kits, and knitting patterns.
buttonandblue.com

•

Anna Maltz is a knit detective, ex-art kid, amateur ice cream enthusiast, colour fancier, Londoner, and maker of many things. She is also Pom Pom's resident columnist.
annamaltz.com

•

Anna Strandberg is 41 years old and lives with her husband and two sons in Stockholm, Sweden. She dyes organic yarns in all kinds of colours under the name Dandelion Yarns. She used to work as an art director, and loves poodles. Luna is her first published pattern.
dandelionyarns.se

•

Carissa Browning lives and knits in Dallas, Texas, where she has accepted the futility of stitching warm woollen sweaters and has perhaps overcompensated with an abundance of handknit socks. She can now last three months without wearing the same pair twice. More of her work can be found at *carissaknits.com*

•

Catherine Clark has been designing knitwear since the age of 16. Her published patterns can be found on Ravelry at ravelry.com/people/brooklyngeneral. Catherine is also the owner of Brooklyn General Store and Bluebird Midwifery, blending her love of craft with her love of community and women's health.

•

Emily Foden is a day-dreaming, moongazing knitter as well as the dyer behind Viola. She lives and works in an old general store in Mooresburg, Ontario, Canada, and draws inspiration from the rural landscape that surrounds her. Emily loves to go for walks with her dog Lucy and is also an avid baker and pebble collector.
violaandthemoon.com

•

Esther Romo Alonso lives in Madrid. She's been knitting for many years and her enthusiasm for textile design increased her knowledge of handweaving. Her day job is as a UX designer in MKT automation. She combines her knowledge from both worlds with a love of technology. Find her on Ravelry, Instagram, and Twitter as *@elleplusdesign* or at *elleplusdesign.com*

Fiona Alice recently left her native home of Nova Scotia, Canada, to begin a new adventure in Finland. Fiona is looking forward to sourcing inspiration for fresh knitwear designs from the new textures and colour palettes that Helsinki has to offer. You can find her at *fionaalice.com* or on Instagram as *@fiona_alice_*

•

Jule Kebelmann studied textile design and worked as a freelance knitwear designer for small fashion labels and films. A favourite project was working on the film *Cloud Atlas*. After years of teaching knitting classes she has started her own yarn business, Hey Mama Wolf, which produces sustainable plant-dyed yarns.
etsy.com/shop/heymamawolfyarns

•

Maddie Harvey is a freelance designer and knitting teacher, living and working in Edinburgh, UK. She loves bold and simple knitwear designs, especially those that use stripes and colourwork in striking colour combinations. A former primary school teacher, Maddie is inspired by colour, geometry, and knitwear construction. Find out more at *maddieharveydesigns.com*

•

Melanie Berg combines texture and colour into wearable modern designs that are both playful and beautiful. She designs to surprise – from matching cheeky stripes with elegant lace, to choosing unexpected colour combinations. She loves to collaborate with other creative types around the world, and her patterns have been published by yarn companies and knitting magazines large and small.
mairlynd.de

•

Rebecca Lawrence is currently pursuing her dream of being a vintner and sommelier, and her freelance work as a recipe developer means she hasn't had to leave out her love of food. When she's not raving about Italian reds, or running food and wine pairing evenings, she can be found in her garden or curled up with her knitting, usually accompanied by a large glass of something.
rosmarinoevino.com

THE MOONROCKS

Our Issue 26 Yarns

Anchor - Artiste Metallic
makeitcoats.com

•

Dandelion Yarns - Rosy Sport
dandelionyarns.se

•

Hey Mama Wolf - Schafwolle No.03
+ Sockyarn No.04
etsy.com/shop/heymamawolfyarns

•

Illimani Yarn - Amelie
illimaniyarn.com

•

Madelinetosh - Pashmina
madelinetosh.com

•

Magpie Fibers - Swanky Sock
magpiefibers.com

•

Shibui Knits - Cima + Silk Cloud
shibuiknits.com

•

The Uncommon Thread - BFL Fingering
theuncommonthread.co.uk

•

Triskelion Yarn - Scylfing DK
triskelion-yarn.com

•

Viola - Mohair Lace
violaandthemoon.com

•

Woollenflower - Masgot Fine + Whorl
woollenflower.com

image by **Emily Foden**